Feltmaking
The Whys and Wherefores

Sheila Smith and Freda Walker

Copyright 1995 Sheila Smith and Freda Walker
First published in 1995 by Dalefelt Publications,
Thirsk, North Yorkshire YO7 4LN
Printed in Great Britain by Maxiprint, York YO3 4XF

ISBN: 0 9527262 0 3

All rights reserved. No part of this publication may be reproduced or transmitted in any form or by any means, electronic, mechanical, photocopying, recording, or any information storage or retrieval system, without the prior permission in writing of the authors.

About the Authors

Sheila Smith
Sheila trained as a teacher of Home Economics and followed this career for over twenty years. In the mid - eighties while studying, as a mature student, for a diploma in Constructed Textile Design she decided as part of her final project, to design and make a jacket made from a combination of felt and knit. She had seen jackets made from felt but all seemed to be stiff and heavy so her aim was to produce a jacket which would be soft and comfortable but hard-wearing. Little did she realise that this was to be the beginning of a fascination with the ancient craft of feltmaking.

She experimented with different methods of making felt and attended workshops with several different feltmakers each one using different methods. She made felt stitched into parcels of cotton sheeting, tied into rolls around drain pipes held in place with the legs of old tights, or around wooden dowels with carefully applied elastic bandages and even kneeling on the floor with the roll of felt in an old zinc bath. The one thing these different methods had in common was that the end result was always a complete surprise as nothing was revealed until the final process was completed.

Sheila decided that there must be other ways of making felt where the feltmaker would be in control of what was happening and able to deal with any faults as they occurred, instead of being disappointed at finding the faults after the felt was made and too late to rectify them.

After almost a year of experimentation the quality of her felt was improving steadily until finally she met Freda who taught her the all important process of milling felt, which is essential to give it the wearing properties needed for garments. She had done it! She had made felt fit for garments and the completed jacket duly appeared at her final show. From that time onwards she has continued experimenting with felt and never ceases to be amazed at its versatility.

Freda Walker
Initially Freda trained as a teacher of Home Economics specialising in Needlework. During her years of teaching she continued to acquire skills in other crafts achieving what she thought was a final ambition, learning to spin and weave.

In 1979, 'The Art Of The Feltmaker' exhibition at Abbot Hall Art Gallery, Kendal, Cumbria became the catalyst that was to set her off on a whole new craft adventure. A subsequent meeting with Peter Walter, who was employed in industrial feltmaking, ensured that she was able fully to understand the principles involved. He became her mentor. It was his initiative that encouraged a small group of hand feltmakers to meet at Bury Cooper & Whitehead's factory where he worked. As a result of this meeting the Feltmakers Association, of which she was a founder member was formed.

As a spinner, Freda was already expert in the handling of carders and had acquired much knowledge of fleece. She specialised in the use of fleece from British sheep breeds using natural coloured wool to best advantage. She soon found that feltmaking had become a full-time occupation, being asked to give demonstrations, lectures and to hold workshops for both children and adults. Magazines requested articles and she exhibited her work widely. Freda's expertise was recognised and she was asked to appear twice on Border Television and on a national programme for Television South.

As well as the results of her own experimentation Freda has collected a wealth of information through her researches. It was auspicious for her to meet Sheila who shares the same enthusiasm and fascination for the subject.

Freda is pleased to pass on the cumulative results of her experience and hope 'Feltmaking - The Whys and Wherefores' will be the inspiration for a new generation of feltmakers.

Acknowledgements

Grateful acknowledgement is made to the British Wool Marketing Board who supplied the samples of fleece for the Felting tests.

All data used has been taken from B. W. M. B. Publications :
'British Sheep and Wool'   1990 edition
'Wool Grade Specifications'   1992 edition
Woolmark

For permission to use cartoons we thank B. W. M. B. and the Women's Royal Voluntary Service ; also I.W.S. for the use of the illustration of the structure of wool fibres.

Foreword

Twenty years ago the title of this book would have attracted little attention. So far had this ancient art disappeared in the West that its occurrence is still being rediscovered in some places. Gradually since 1979 feltmaking is being revived once more all over the world. Feltmakers are not only pioneering the practice but writing books to spread the word. Last year a new important book in Denmark, next year one in Poland and now in England we have 'Feltmaking , the Whys and Wherefores' from, appropriately, Kendal. The authors are Freda Walker and Sheila Smith, the former from Kendal and the latter from Thirsk.

From my first encounter with felt in Gumbad-i-Qubus in 1962 it had taken until 1979 to put on the exhibition 'The Art of the Feltmaker'. At that time Freda Walker was one of the first people to be excited by it all. She has never stopped and she and her friend Sheila, also a practising feltmaker, pooled their knowledge and expertise to write this invaluable book.

The amazing fact which Speakman recorded in 1994, that wool fibres which had lain in a drawer for twenty years had spontaneously felted is enough to explain the 'magic' which was attached to feltmaking in ancient times. It reminds me of the day in 1979 when at Abbott Hall, 'The Art of the Feltmaker' show had just opened, announced on the main road through Kendal by A.A. signs. Peter Walter, then working at Bury, Cooper Whiteheads' felt factory came rushing in to see me and asked almost antagonistically 'What's this exhibition about felt all about ?' He had never encountered oriental felt, I had never heard of Bury, Cooper, Whitehead or visited his factory. Gradually he calmed down as we looked at the exhibition and then he told me a lovely story.

I said 'Why are you so excited about felt, working in a factory?' His answer was that felt was alive. He'd had to take a piece of black felt to Birmingham to a client. It was black on one side and white on the other. The train was late. It was pouring with rain - he ran from the station holding the piece of felt in his pocket. Soaking wet, he produced it for the client. To his horror it was black and white on one side and white and black on the other. 'You see it had gone on working' he explained. He loved his work and played an important part in the founding of the Feltmakers' Association.

Mary Burkett O.B.E.
Former Director, Abbott Hall, Kendal.
President International Feltmakers' Association

Contents

Sheep and Wool in History 1

What is Felt? 4

Fibres and Feltabilty 8

The Crimp Factor. 15

Making Hand-rolled Felt 19

Further Techniques. 28

Three-Dimensional Felt. 35

Making Cones and Capelines for Hat Making. 40

Felt for Garments. 50

Testing Fleece for Feltability 51

Record Keeping 56

Summary for the Serious Student 58

Bibliography 62

Glossary. 65

Useful Addresses 72

Introduction

This book is intended to give prospective feltmakers the information necessary to enable them to make the quality of felt which suits their own particular purpose.

Ideas and ways in which felt may be used are given in order to illustrate its versatility but it is not intended as a recipe book but rather as a catalyst to encourage the feltmaker to experiment and use their own ideas.

Sheep and Wool in History

There is little evidence other than fossils and fossilised remains found in Central Asia to indicate the origins of sheep. Certainly their beginnings were pre-historic. Ancient drawings and sculptures are an indication of what they would have looked like, some having two, four or six horns. The domestication of sheep appears to have occurred about 10,000 BC. The dog was probably already domesticated and these two animals still have a close working relationship. There is nothing 'woolly - headed' about sheep when they are wise enough to grow a coat which can protect them from the elements - heat, cold, rain and wind. When man first killed sheep for food he would have realised these important characteristics and used the skins to protect himself - but killing the sheep was unnecessarily wasteful and led to the domestication of the animals.

The domestication of feral sheep enabled man to have milk which is particularly important for nomadic tribes; providing liquid and a valuable food source. He would have observed that sheep moulted naturally in Spring and early Summer and was, therefore, able to pluck the fleece to obtain wool for spinning. Even in this century 'rooing' the fleece is a method used in the Shetlands. The primitive breed Soay is a small hardy sheep in the Hebrides which sheds its fleece annually. As a result of domestication and breeding , sheep are now clipped annually but this still happens in early summer 'when the wool rises', as if in preparation for moulting.

A requirement of domestication is to control the breeding of sheep, so man learned to select. Genesis, xxx, 32, describes how Jacob removes the 'speckled and spotted and all the brown' from Laban's flock. Verse 40 quotes, 'And Jacob did separate the lambs'. Today's sheep breeds are the result of centuries of selective breeding. Speckled and coloured fleece are still found today, e.g. Jacob (speckled). Hebridean (black) and Manx Loghtan (brown).

Ancient Greek mythology tells us the story of Jason who ventured to find the Golden Fleece. There are differing explanations for the colour, one being that it was embroidered with gold thread. There are references to yellow wool in Mesopotamia and Egypt; probably brought there from Asia Minor by the Phoenicians who had established a wool trade circa 500 BC. An interesting explanation is of more recent origin (1984). A photograph taken in the Caucasus shows how sheepskins are used to trap particles of gold borne down by mountain streams. As the water flows over the fleece the metal sticks in the wool making it literally glitter with gold. The Romans who came to England in 55 BC encouraged the breeding of sheep to improve the quality of fleece for spinning and the manufacture of yarn into cloth. Important Romans wore togas made from fine quality cloth. This cloth was traditionally whitened with chalk at election times when the candidates wished to stand out in the crowds of similarly clothed listeners. In Latin the word 'candidatus' means 'white-robed'.

After the Norman Conquest much of the land was owned by the great abbeys and farmed by peasant tenants, servants or lay brothers. Monks were astute business men who did much to further the establishment of the wool trade and became experts in the selective breeding of sheep. The Domesday Survey 1085-6 lists 13,000 sheep owned by Ely Abbey. Furness Abbey was exporting fleece to Calais by boat, two of which were owned for this purpose. By the end of the thirteenth century Fountains Abbey was producing more than 28,000lb of wool each year.

The Black Death in 1349 so reduced the population that there were insufficient workers to maintain agriculture. Requiring fewer workers, the rearing of sheep therefore took precedence on the land which had once been cultivated. So wool-growing became a major source of work, income and wealth. Successive monarchs used the flourishing woollen industry as a source of income by laws and taxation. Elizabeth I decreed in 1571 that woollen caps had to be worn by all ; another law of 1667 decreed that all persons should be buried in woollen cloth, with a penalty of £5 for not doing so.

This heritage is perpetuated by the tradition of the Lord Chancellor sitting upon the Woolsack when in the House of Lords during Parliamentary sessions. The Woolsack is a large cushion made from red cloth stuffed with wool, symbolising the wealth of the country. Wool bales were transported by pack-horse in medieval times and would weigh about 250lb and contain approximately 100 tightly packed fleece. In 1965 the Woolsack was refilled with new wool provided by the B.W.M.B. and from fourteen Commonwealth countries who held a conference in London that year. The Woolsack is believed to date from the reign of Elizabeth I but there is prior evidence of the custom from 1539 when Henry VIII decreed : Such as them as shall happen to be under the said degree of a Baron shall sit at the uppermost parts of the sakes in the middle of the said Parliament Chamber'.

A ransom paid for the freedom of Richard I from an Austrian prison was reputed to have been paid with wool. I think, however, it would have been silver raised as taxes on wool. Likewise the Old London Bridge was reputed to be built on wool - not literally - but with revenue raised when wool was exported.

The Industrial Revolution in the nineteenth century was a time of major social change as it brought about the demise of the cottage industry. Factories now dominated the sky-line and families were separated by their work. Local cottage industries were transformed into large-scale businesses where machinery replaced the hand-skills learned through generations. Over the centuries there were fluctuations in the woollen trade and it became less important in some areas whilst flourishing in others.

Many products became known by their area of origin or fleece used. Harris tweed, Swaledale and Herdwick tweeds, Otterburn rugs, Witney blankets and Welsh tapestry. The Bradford area gave us the 'Bradford Count' and is still noted for quality worsted cloth.

Spanning thousands of years, the story of sheep and wool has given us a wealth of history including social, legal, language, clothing and folk-lore. Wealthy merchants paid architects to build 'Wool Churches' which can be seen today mainly in southern England. The parish church of Saint Peter and Saint Paul in Lavenham, Suffolk is a beautiful and well-preserved example. Rebuilt in the fifteenth century, the finance was provided by local clothiers who organised the trade from wool to cloth. Lavenham, itself, is well worth visiting as it has retained much of its medieval history in buildings and nomenclature associated with wool and cloth production. John Barton, stapler of Holme near Newark recorded in stained glass - 'I thank God and ever shall. It is the sheepe hath payed for all'.

The whole textile industry underwent a second revolution in the twentieth century with the development of a new breed of fibres, the 'synthetics' which were heralded as the replacement for natural fibres. They had certain disadvantages in their use for clothing, but by careful blending with natural fibres, yarns exhibiting the best characteristics of both have been achieved. For a while the production of synthetic fibres did affect the wool trade. It soon recovered both due to good marketing and to the discovery of a method to make woollen yarns shrink-resistant and thus garments which are 'machine washable'. The one drawback of wool has been its tendency to matt and felt if not washed with great care. The Feltmaker, of course, encourages this disadvantage.

What is Felt?

Felt has been defined as "a textile structure composed entirely of fibres physically interlocked and consolidated by the use of mechanical work, chemical action and moisture without the use of weaving, knitting, stitching, thermal bonding or adhesives". In layman's terms this means that wool fibres are felted by the application of heat, moisture and friction. This can be illustrated accidentally when washing a woollen sweater - if the water is too hot or the sweater is agitated too vigorously it will shrink and no amount of stretching will return it to its original size.

The Textile Institute in its 'Textile Terms and Definitions' 1991 divides felt into three different catagories - these are:
1. pressed felt formed from a web of animal hair or wool which is consolidated by moisture, heat and mechanical action.
2. woven or knitted felts formed from staple fibre fabrics which have some wool content - these are subjected to the same processes as in category 1 to such a degree that the original fabric construction is completely obscured by the smooth felted surface.
3. needlefelt is a non-woven structure formed by the mechanical bonding of a fibre web by needling (the use of barbed needles in a needleboard). Felting needles are mounted in a board in densities of 300 - 500 needles per square metre. Several thin layers of fibres are passed under the needle board and as the needles are lowered they pass through the fibres and as they are raised the barbs in the needles pull fibres from the lower layers up through fibres in the upper layers. This process is repeated many times at speed and as the fibres pass under the needles they are formed into a continuous web.

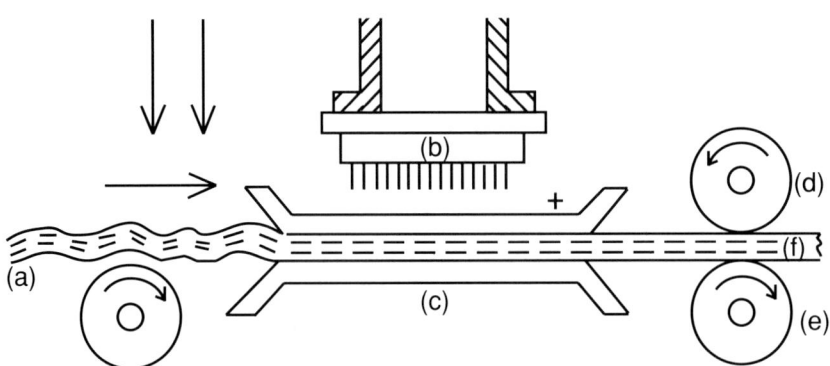

(a) web of fibre (b) needleboard with barbed needles
(c) bed plate (d) pressing rollers
(e) draw rollers (f) felt

History of Felt

Wool felt is the earliest known form of textile fabric and played an important part in the life of early man. Throughout central Asia, where some of the oldest felts have been found, Turkoman nomads made their tents, clothes and floor coverings from the material and it consequently became a significant part of many religious rituals. Brides were seated on white felt during marriage ceremonies and animals were sacrificed on it. It was also believed to have magical properties - Mongolian horsemen would hang felt figures inside their tents to bring good luck and to ward off evil spirits and a felt mattress would protect the sleeper from dangerous snakes and scorpions. Feltmaking was also illustrated as a technical process in Roman times in the mural paintings of the Fuller's House in Pompeii.

Legendary origins of felt have been handed down in each feltmaking country but the true origin of felt is unknown. One amusing legend tells of St.Clement "Patron Saint of Hatters" who was being pursued by his enemies. As he ran his feet became increasingly hot and painful, but he managed to give his pursuers the slip and stopped to gather some sheep's wool which he saw entangled in the bushes. He wrapped the wool around his feet and placing his feet back into his sandals proceeded speedily on his way. When he finally arrived at his destination he removed his sandals and found that the wool had felted due to the heat and perspiration from his feet.

Archaeologists have unearthed fragments of felt dating back to the Bronze Age. The most exciting examples were discovered earlier this century when stone burial chambers in the Altai Mountains of Siberia were opened. These burial chambers were of chieftains of ancient nomadic tribes who populated this area between the seventh and second centuries BC. The methods which had been used to construct the tombs and the severe climate of the High Altai had caused a layer of frozen ground to form under the large cairns which covered the graves. The Altai tombs have achieved world wide fame because, being completely frozen, they preserved items made of organic materials which under normal conditions would have been destroyed by the passage of time. Amongst the finds were items of fur and leather, felt and textile, as well as wood carvings, all of which retained their original form and colour.

The ancient inhabitants of the Altai produced fine leather which was used for appliqué work, they used several different stitches in decorative work and felt was made from both coarse and fine sheep's wool in different densities, qualities and thicknesses for items of everyday use but also for art. Their art was decorative, ornate and colourful - taking vegetable, animal and geometrical designs as their inspiration.

Some thirty different types of felt items were found - these included felt rugs, tomb covers, socks and cushions - most are heavily patterned. The largest piece measured 4.5 x 6.5 metres - this is now known as the Pazyryk felt and is housed in the Hermitage Museum in St. Petersburg.

Felt is not now a common product in the West apart from industrial uses although it was used extensively in the hatting industry in England until the nineteenth century. Scandinavia also had early traditions of feltmaking but these have died out as a home industry.

An interest in hand-rolled felt has recently revived and the possibilities of felt are being explored for use in garments and for decorative purposes. Because feltmaking is no longer a necessity of everyday life the craftsman can concentrate on fashion and decoration rather than utility. Craftsmen of other disciplines can introduce their own interpretations using skills already mastered. Spinners and weavers in particular take to felting because they already understand the nature and preparation of fibres. College students now produce exciting examples of felt and use it imaginatively. So to the Ancient History we can add a modern Revivalist Movement. Hopefully this book will encourage and inspire, and ensure that feltmaking not only has a past but a future.

Industrial Feltmaking and its Uses

Felt differs in density and quality depending on the type of wool fibres used. The strength of the felt is controlled by the number of layers of fibres and the degree of fulling. Transverse strength is built up by cross layering the fibres and the strength between the layers relies on the degree of hardening and fulling that the felt is subjected to. In general the longer the fulling process is continued the tighter the fibres interlock and the greater the density of the felt. The denser the felt the harder it becomes but hardness is also dependent on the quality and type of wool fibres used.

Industrial Felt Manufacture
Differences in the origin and type of wool, in the fibre fineness, degree of crimp and the extent of fibre weathering all lead to differences in felting behaviour. Among the best wools for speed of felting are Merino wools from Australia and South Africa.

What industrial felt is used for
Felt is a versatile fabric and can be produced in weights and densities to suit different end uses. It is durable and light in weight and for these reasons it is widely used in industry. In a fairly thin and lightweight form it is used as an interlining to add body to outerwear garments, to line jewellery cases, as base coverings for table lamps and for billiard and card table tops.

The display trade use it extensively for exhibition stands and shop window fittings. It is now more cost effective and convenient to cover large areas with felt than it is to paint them. No time is lost in waiting for the paint to dry so that backgrounds for exhibitions can be constructed rapidly out of felt and meet the tight schedules demanded by the industry.

Piano manufactures use felt as pads for each of the eighty five keys on a piano and felt pieces have been known to perform in pianos for over eighty years and retain their original tonal qualities with no maintenance other than normal cleaning and tuning of the instrument.

Heavy industry also uses felt as pads in machinery and as covers for polishing discs.

The processes in making industrial felt
1. Formation of a batt of firm uniform thickness and density.
2. Hardening - the first consolidation or felting process in which warm, moist fibres are subjected to a combination of pressure and shaking forces.
3. Fulling or milling completes the consolidation and shrinkage by pressure and friction from fulling stocks (hammers) or rotary milling machines.
4. Finishing treatments such as pressing and shearing may be carried out depending on the end use of the felt.

Fibres and Feltability

It is surely magical that the soft, springy fibres of wool can by a simple process be transformed into felt; felt which can be soft and fine but also so thick that it can be cut into solid blocks resembling bricks. For the hand-felter this transformation from fibres to a felt fabric does not require any equipment as for weaving. It is romantic to think that magic plays a part and there are some apocryphal stories but there are, of course, sound scientific explanations.

Animal fibres are uniquely suitable for the production of felt. Although they can vary greatly in appearance they all have common factors. They are all protein in origin this being called keratin; they have a variable wavy appearance known as crimp; each fibre is covered with overlapping scales. These scales are an essential factor for felting and are only present in animal fibres. Some animal hair fibres such as rabbit, muskrat and beaver must undergo a complex chemical process known as carroting to enable them to felt. This process produces excellent felts and has been used successfully in the hat industry for many years. Wool from sheep, however, felts very easily when subjected to moisture, heat and friction whilst the addition of an alkali, e.g. soap solution also facilitates the process. Locks of wool can vary greatly in length from the 3cm of Southdown to the Lincoln Longwool which can measure up to 35cm. Industrial felters advise a staple i.e. length, of about 7cm but longer fibres can give interesting results for the hand feltmaker. Fibres which are too short, however, will create potential difficulties in preparation of the batt when the overlapping of layers is required.

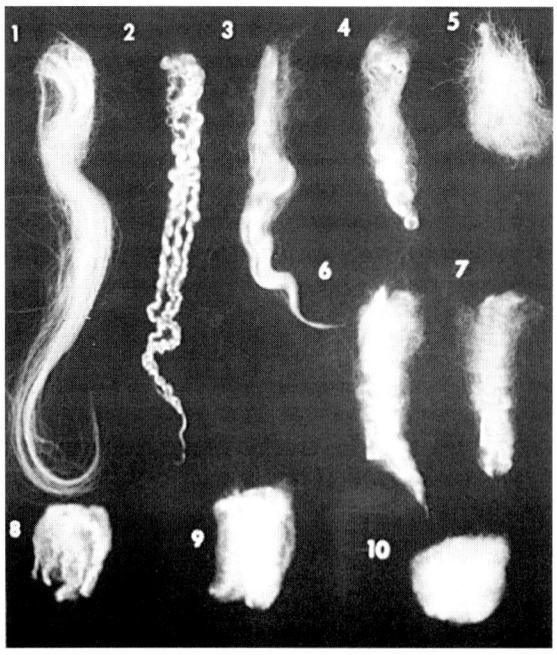

1. Scottish Blackface
2. Wensleydale
3. Lincoln Longwood
4. Masham
5. Welsh Mountain
6. Border Leicester
7. Romney
8. Merino
9. Kerry Hill
10. Suffolk

The staple length not only varies with the breed of sheep but can have a different appearance and quality within the area of the individual fleece. The areas of the shoulders and back being of better quality than the outer areas.

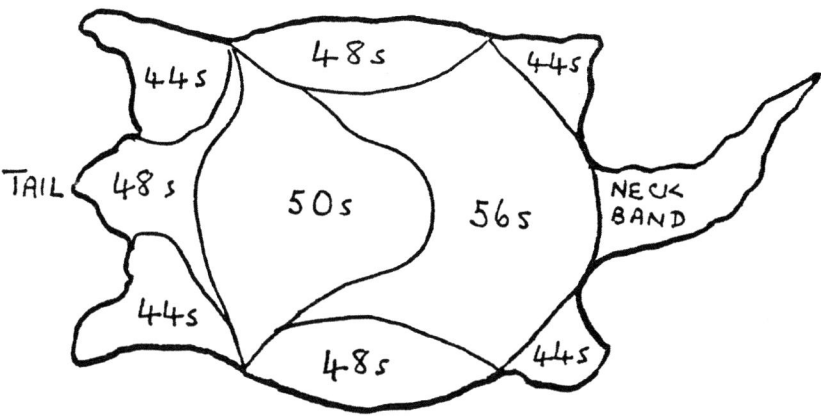

The *higher* numbers indicate *better* quality.
The *lower* numbers indicate *poorer* quality.

Fibre thickness is a deciding factor of quality. The traditional measurement of quality of wool developed in Bradford is based on the number of skeins, each consisting of 560 yards of yarn (spun worsted) which can be produced from 1lb of wool. The number of skeins becomes the count and can range between 28s and 100s. Merino, the main breed in Australia, is of very fine quality and can be in the range of 60s - 100s. This is not a native British breed, being originally from Spain, but some 'English' Merino is now available and is of importance to the feltmaker. A pound of Merino producing 80 skeins is known as being 80s count Herdwick producing perhaps 30 skeins is thus a 30s count category. These are two extreme examples, the majority of grades falling in the categories 48s - 58s. Of historical interest is that handspinners used to be paid using the count system i.e. the number of hanks they had spun as a calculating basis. The expertise of wool grading has developed by experience with skills passing from generation to generation. Although modern spinning techniques do allow coarser fibres to be spun into finer yarns the count system remains the recognised standard. The British Wool Marketing Board produces a catalogue of 'Wool Grade Specifications' examples of which are quoted in the tables of information at the back of the book. Skeins and yarns may seem to be a peculiar measurement for a feltmaker to use, i.e. yarn related rather than fibre. It does however give an accurate guidance to the quality of the fibres themselves.

For those who like a scientific challenge and have the use of a microscopic ruler, fibre thickness can be measured in microns. One micron is a millionth of a metre.
The finest fibres (80s quality) measure 17 microns across.
The medium fibres (58s quality) measure 26 microns across.
The coarse fibres (40s quality) measure 37 microns across.

Approximate Relationship : Bradford Count to Average Fibre Diameter

Quality Numbers	40/44s	46s	50s	56s	60s	64s	66s	70s	80s	90s
Microns	37	33	30	28	24	22	20	18	17	16

Wool Growers of New Zealand and Australia use the micron measurement for quality as they do not have the great variety of breeds found in the British Isles. The Merino types all fall into a narrow, high quality range. For the hand feltmaker the Bradford Count is the easiest and most reliable guide to quality.

The microscopic examination of wool fibres clearly shows them to be covered with overlapping scales. Coarse fibres have large flat scales whilst the finer fibres have a much smaller scale structure.

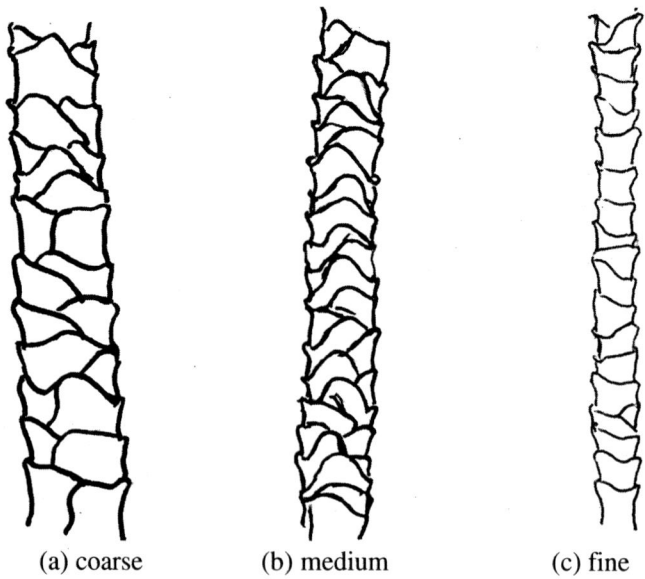

(a) coarse (b) medium (c) fine

The size of the scales is also linked to the crimp (the visible waviness) of the fibres. In general the more crimp that is present, the smaller are the scales and the finer is the wool.

Locks of Wool Fibres

Masham
Medium Wavy

Suffolk
Fine Crimped

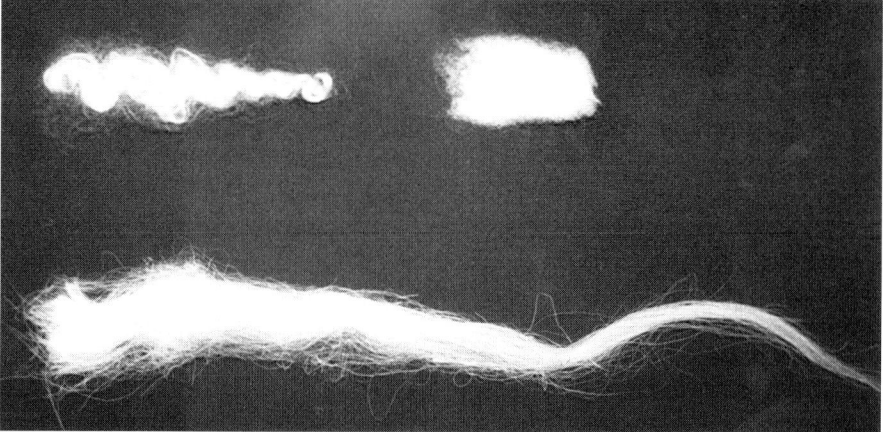

Scottish Blackface
Coarse Straight

Knowledge of this scale structure is essential to the understanding of why wool felts. The scales are each fastened at the base to the core of the fibre and are free at the edges. Because the scales overlap towards the tip of each fibre they help to prevent foreign matter from working into the fleece thus minimising damage. In combination with the natural grease present, lanolin, they direct the shedding of rain water from the fleece.

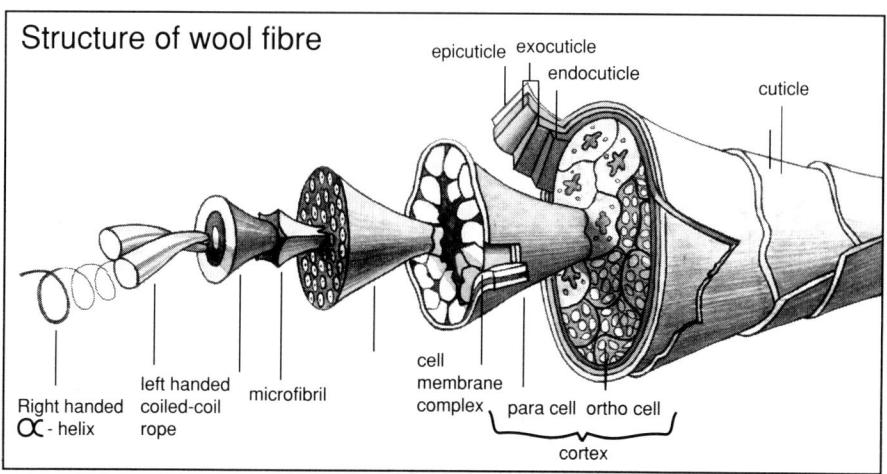

It is the outer scale covering which is the vital component which, under certain conditions, causes wool to felt. Anyone who has accidentally put a woollen garment in a washing machine on a hot setting will know to their cost that wool can shrink dramatically. The first attempts to prevent shrinkage used chemicals to remove the tips of the scales but this process, chlorination, affected the quality of the wool and was only partially successful. Modern developments have produced a machine-washable wool by covering the scales with a silicone-based polymer which has the result of making the wool smoother. Smooth, straight fibres tend to slip past each other and therefore do not felt. This was achieved without detriment to the wool.

Now that we have proof of this anti-shrink process it confirms it is the scaliness of wool fibres which is the primary cause of felting. This visible characteristic should be examined further. Take one of your own hairs with the root visible and rub it lengthways between thumb and first finger and observe the result. If a fibre is pulled between finger and thumb tip first, then a resistance is felt; if pulled root first the fingers slip over the surface. The friction is therefore greater when applied tip to root. It is this friction which pushes the fibre towards the root end. If the fibre is free then it migrates uni-directionally; should it be held at the root end by another fibre then it bends under the friction. This reduces the distance from tip to root. When this happens to fibres in a fabric then it shows as shrinkage.

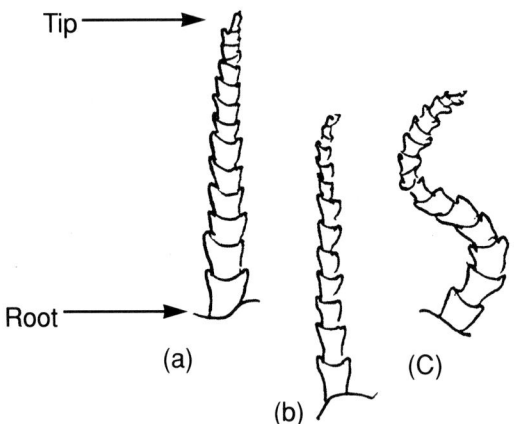

(a) Fibre in original position
(b) Fibre free to move root first
(c) Fibre unable to move - bends

The difference in friction of the movement root to tip and tip to root is known as directional frictional effect or D.F.E.
So in any mass of fibres prepared as for felting there could be some moving uni-directionally and some curling and bending.

The preparation for felting involves carding to separate the fibres which are cross-layered into a thick batt. The separation allows space for each fibre to move when being worked initially; the cross-layering places the root-tip orientation in different directions. When moisture and friction is applied, encouraged by the use of an alkali (soap or detergent) the fibre movement towards the root is activated. Only a proportion of the fibres are moving at any one time through those which are not affected by the direction of the friction.

It could be argued that the maximum shrinkage should occur when a circular movement is used, thus giving the maximum number of fibre movements. Rolling forward and backwards is the most common method used but care has to be taken to roll the piece evenly in all directions otherwise a square will become an oblong and a circle an oval. For students and those who like to experiment this could be an interesting exercise. Proof of the migration of fibres can be shown by making up a batt with two layers of white fibres and then two layers of black. When this is felted it will be noticed that the white side should be flecked with black fibres and vice-versa. Peter Walter tells of an occasion when this actually happened to two pieces of felt (white and black) which he was carrying in his pocket. He was hurrying to keep a business appointment and was surprised to find that the friction created in his pocket had caused some of the fibres to transfer - black to white, white to black.

Wool is the general term used for the fibres of a fleece but close inspection can reveal differences in appearance in some breeds. Fibres are classified as being wool, hair or kemp. When all three types are present they grow in regular group patterns in the skin. Kemp is the name given to the easily recognisable, whitish fibres which are short, coarse and brittle. They differ in cellular arrangement from wool in that up to 90% of the central area can be medulla. Medulla cells have porous channels filled with air and lacking in solid substance which accounts for the brittleness of the kemp. In quality wool cortex cells predominate with only a small central section of medulla. In very high quality wool, e.g. Merino, medulla is absent altogether.

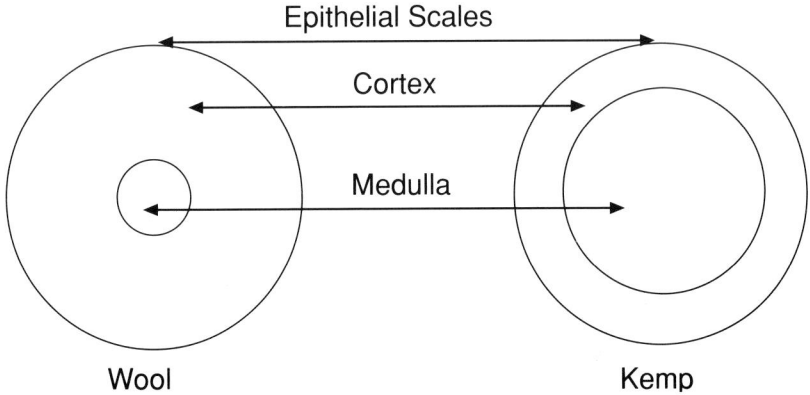

Kemp fibres are not very absorbent, resist dyeing and do not contribute to the strength of felt. Although they have good D.F.E. they lack the crimp and pliability necessary for successful felting. They can, however, contribute to surface texture but tend to loosen and shed. Kempy fleeces are therefore restricted in their uses. Mountain breeds such as Rough Fell, Scottish Blackface, Swaledale and Herdwick are likely to be 'kempy'. The wild ancestor of domestic sheep had a double coat consisting of longer hairs over an undercoat of shorter wool. These longer hairs are coarser and straighter than wool fibres; their purpose being to shed rain water whilst the woolly undercoat provides warmth. Selective breeding has reduced the predominance of hair and encouraged the growth of quality wool such as the Downs breeds with a short staple. Contrasting in length are the Longwool and Lustre breeds which also have hair present. It should be noted that hair and kemp can sometimes be found in the areas of the hind quarters and legs even when absent from the fleece itself.

With thirty four main breeds from which to select a fleece, twelve minor breeds, eight rare breeds and eight half-breeds, the hand feltmaker has a wealth of natural material to work with. Understanding the fundamental reasons for feltability and the fibre qualities necessary should help your choice. The easy option of course is to buy already prepared wool tops, natural or dyed. But if you want a challenge and excitement then choose your own fleece and have it under your control from the beginning. You will soon learn which fibres give you the best results. Experience will also teach you how to choose the fibres which are most suitable for the purposes for which the felt is ultimately to be used. When you can do this successfully then you can claim the title 'Feltmaker'.

The Crimp Factor

Crimp is the distinctive feature of wool fibres, although it is absent from those of a more hairy nature. As early as 1837 three textile scientists realised the important part that crimp played in the felting process of wool fibres. They also decided that the tendency of wool to curl and become entangled played a part. However they missed what is now considered to be the essential factor in felting - the influence of the fibre scales. Burgess in 1867 considered that scales were responsible for the ability to felt but rejected the idea in favour of the crimp factor. By 1953 R W Moncrieff states that "opinion is that crimp plays a part, although probably not a major part in the felting of wool". It should however be noted that rayon manufacturers insert crimp artificially if the rayon is to be mixed with wool in some commercial felts. The fibre structure is thus compatible for processing.

An understanding of crimp formation is a prerequisite to good feltmaking. By understanding the medium you can begin to comprehend and control fully the process and thus the quality of the finished felt. Crimp is seen as the waviness of the fibre but in fact it is a coiled, spiral formation.

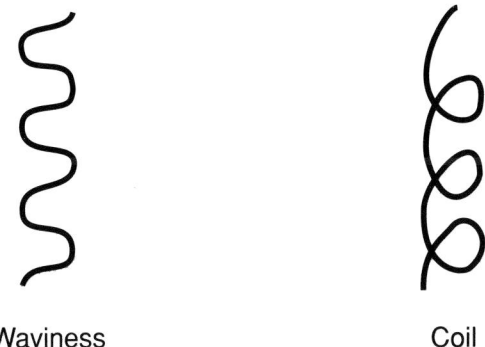

Fig. 1   Waviness   Coil

Because of this coiled structure, wool fibres can be stretched and when released they return to their original length. This elasticity means that the fibres have good recovery and this movement is an important factor in felting.

On examination crimp has both a measurement of amplitude and frequency. Amplitude is the size of the individual loop ; frequency is the spacing between loops. Imagine a coiled spring being slightly pulled out so that each loop is separated and this most easily explains these terms.

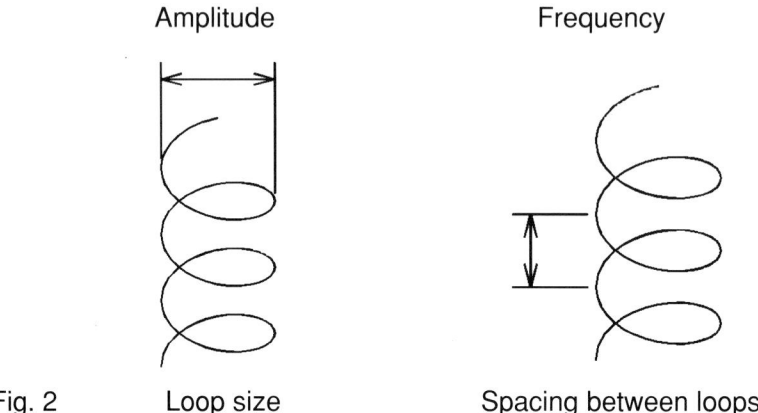

Fig. 2   Loop size   Spacing between loops

The greater the crimp amplitude the larger the loops. The greater the crimp frequency the closer together are the loops. Peter Walter writes "In general, the smaller the loop size (amplitude) and the higher the crimp frequency (more loops) the better the fibre felts". Thus a fine Merino with its pronounced crimp would be expected to felt more easily than a coarse Herdwick with less noticeable crimp.

Estimate of Crimp per cm

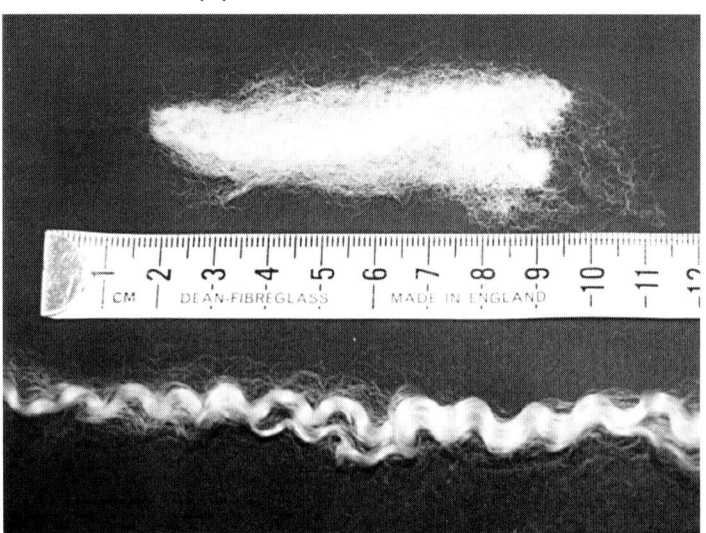

Fig.3

Although feltmaking requires no spinning or weaving to create a fabric, both methods have a common preparation, i.e. Carding. It is interesting to find a reference to the crimpy nature of wool by Catullus who was an early Roman poet and contemporary of Julius Caesar; "The laden distaff in the left hand placed, with springy coils of snow - white wool was graced ...." So his observance of women spindle-spinning resulted in the description of 'springy coils of wool'. For those interested in spinning, this poem is a most accurate and lyrical description of the process.

The 'springy coils' are the result of the physical structure of each wool fibre. A more scientific explanation of the curling of fibres can be proved by microscopic examination. Each fibre is of unequal composition along its length. There are the orthocortex and the paracortex. If the fibre is stained in such a way that only the orthocortex acquires colour, then this bilateral structure can be readily seen under the microscope - fig. 4 (c)

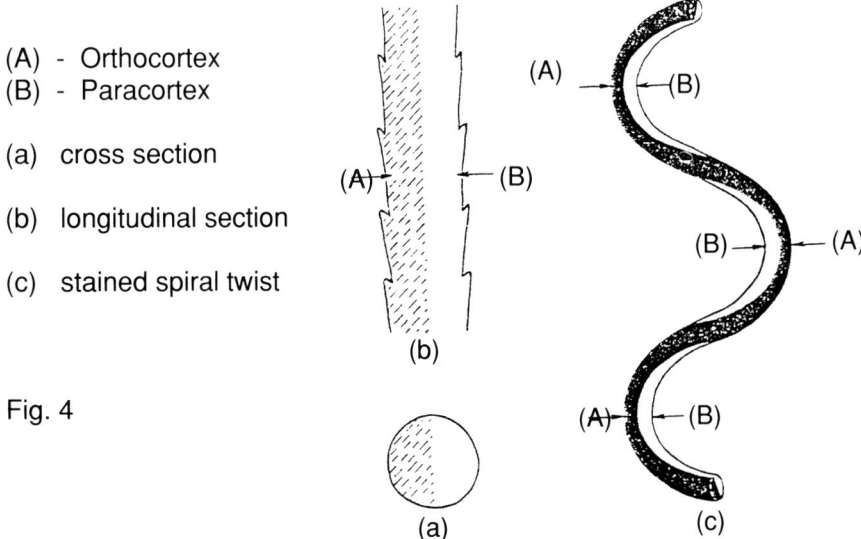

(A) - Orthocortex
(B) - Paracortex

(a) cross section

(b) longitudinal section

(c) stained spiral twist

Fig. 4

Diagram (c) shows the spiral twisting of the combined orthocortex and paracortex of crimped wool. The slightly different physical and chemical structure of A and B results in this formation.

The orthocortex is always on the outside while the paracortex is always on the inside of each crimp curve.

Crimp is difficult to measure if one thinks in terms of crimps per centimetre, although this measurement is used in New Zealand and Australia for the grading of fleece. Not having the wide variety of sheep breeds that are found in the United Kingdom they do not have the equally wide range of grading measurements which we know as the Bradford count. There is a very practical way for feltmakers to arrive at a figure using the difference between the fibre lengths - relaxed and then stretched. For the purpose of this exercise the difference has been converted into a percentage thus giving figures which are easily converted, understood and compared.

R = relaxed measurement   S = stetched measurement   E = extension

S - R = E

% crimp factor = $\frac{E}{R}$ x 100

The crimp factor allows for pockets of air within the structure, these resulting in efficient insulation properties. It must be remembered that natural wool fibres do not have a crimp which remains constant. The curliness of these fibres can vary with both temperature and moisture. This is not surprising when you consider the reasons for animals growing wool in the first place. When the temperature falls the fibres become more bulky to trap more air to keep the animal warm. The crimp thus increases. When fibres become wet they straighten to allow the water to run off and so the crimp level decreases. These fluctuations go some way to explaining the effect of temperature and water when felting. They also help to explain what all breeders and buyers of fleece know as 'cotting'. Wool fibres are always reacting to the weather and atmosphere and could be said to be 'alive'. Whether still on the animal's back or not its fibres continue to lengthen and shorten and in that process rub against each other. Describing the results of this Mabel Ross writes "the fleece of sheep who have suffered a long wet Spring can literally be turned into felt near the skin - this is known as being cotted". Textile scientists use the term 'spontaneous felting'. In 1994 Speakman reported an example of spontaneous felting, attributing this to the repeated extensions and contractions of wool fibres which had undergone a succession of changes of humidity. The fibres in question had lain in a drawer untouched for twenty years. The length movement of the fibres would create a certain friction against each other. Although it had happened very slowly, Speakman records that the fibres had felted.

And so it is that feltmakers can use this natural characteristic of crimp, its movement and extensibility. By applying moisture and physical friction in a controlled manner the feltmaker can speed up the natural tendency of wool to felt.

Making Hand-Rolled Felt

The craft of feltmaking is such an ancient one that there is no one way which could be described as being the correct way to make felt. Over its long history in different parts of the world variations of the basic process have been used. Modern feltmakers gradually develop their own techniques based on the old methods and on the essential factors which are required, i.e. moisture and friction with the addition of heat.

Feltmaking is a very physical activity and requires the input of a fair amount of energy - nothing can be more demoralising than to expend time and effort in trying to produce felt and then to find that the results are not what you expected. An understanding of the fundamental process of felting is essential, careful study of techniques and then the confidence to make an informed choice of fibre depending on the required end result.

It is best for a newcomer to feltmaking to begin by making several small samples before launching into a large project. In this way knowledge is built up, especially if notes and records are kept of fibres, quantities and methods used. 'Why samples?' - some of you will ask. The answer is that sampling is a valuable way of preparing a body of information which will be invaluable and help to prevent disappointment and wasted time.

Choice of Fibres
Wool fibres felt more easily than any other fibres and certain wool fibres felt more easily than others.

For comparisons see felt tests, etc. and table of results on page 52.

The would-be feltmaker will find it easier to begin with combed wool 'tops'. Tops are produced commercially from raw wool fibres and are part of the process of preparing wool for spinning into worsted yarn.. The wool is first 'scoured' or washed to remove dirt and grease, dried and then put through a series of machines which gradually 'card' the fibres so that they are opened out and formed into a continuous rope. The rope is then combed to remove the short fibres. The long ones are left in the form of a thick but untwisted rope with the fibres lying parallel to each other - this is known as a 'top'. When choosing wool tops a good quality such as Merino will guarantee good felting properties.

Equipment required for making hand-rolled felt

Old towels
Length of dowel
Cotton sheeting
Plastic jug
Rubber gloves
Hand carders

Rush or bamboo matting
Net
Plastic spray bottle
Waterproof apron
Felting board

Old towels
Old towels are required as a base to work on and to absorb any excess water. Contrary to general opinion it is not necessary to have the workplace awash with water when making felt! The towels should be placed on the table or worktop area to be used and folded so that they do not hang over the edge. This is important as if they do hang over they will act as a wick and the water will drip to the floor.

Rush or bamboo mats
Rush or bamboo mats are used to provide a textured surface on which to lay the wool fibres ready for felting. The texture of the mat increases the rate of felting. Bamboo mats have more texture than rush ones and consequently are better but are more expensive and not always easy to obtain - either is quite satisfactory. Rush mats are often sold as beach mats and are sold at the seaside while bamboo mats are often intended to be blinds. (You have to remove the fittings). The advantage of bamboo mats for the dedicated feltmaker is that they are available in a variety of widths. The size of mat required depends on the size of felt to be made - the mat should be larger than the felt to be made.

Length of dowel
Length of dowel approximately 1 - 1.5 inches in diameter and should be longer than the measurements of the felt to be made. Broom handles are ideal and rolling pins can be used for small pieces. The dowel provides a rigid centre when rolling the fibres in the bamboo mat.

Net
Net should be larger than the felt to be made. Lightweight synthetic curtain net is ideal. A fairly open mesh should be chosen.

Cotton sheeting
Sheeting should be larger than the felt to be made. Old cotton tea-towels are ideal for small pieces.

Plastic spray bottle
This should be of the plant spray type.

Plastic jug
Used to hold hot water and to fill the spray bottle.

Apron and rubber gloves
For protection.

Surface with ridges
A ridged sink draining board is ideal but if not available there are alternatives such as :
a) Large greenhouse gravel tray with ridged base and no drainage holes.
b) Washboard - old fashioned glass type.
c) Felting board - this can be purchased specially but has the disadvantage of being rather small.
d) Home-made felting board - this is made from a piece of plywood with strips of half dowel pinned in place. The surface should then be sealed with two coats of clear yacht varnish. This is quite inexpensive to make and can be any size. *see diagram*

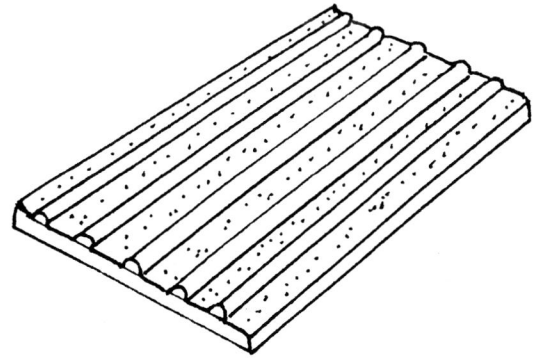

Hand carders
Hand carders are very useful for blending coloured fibres.

To Make Felt

Materials required :
1. *Wool fibres* - these may either be in the form of fleece or combed wool tops. If fleece is used then it must be prepared by scouring to remove the greaseand dirt and then carded either on hand carders or a drum carder. Combed wool tops are prepared commercially - the fibres are scoured and combed so that all fibres are lying in the same direction and at the same time all short fibres are removed. Wool tops are available prepared from many different fleece types - for good felting properties Merino tops are excellent.
2. *Hot water*
3. *Washing up liquid*

When making felt for the first time it is important to make several samples before embarking on a larger project. To make felt successfully it is necessary to be in complete control at every stage - by making samples and keeping careful records you can build up a body of information on which to draw when making a piece of felt which is intended for a specific purpose.

It is good practice to get into the habit of completing a record sheet for every piece of felt which you make. In this way you have a ready reference as to results when contemplating later projects.

To make a felt sample approximately 60cm x 60cm :
Collect together the following equipment : Bamboo mat - large enough for the felt.
Broom handle
Old towels
Piece of net curtaining
Cotton fabric
Spray bottle
Washing up liquid
Combed tops - dyed and undyed
64s Merino good for felting

Method :
There are four distinct processes in making a piece of hand - rolled felt :
a) Laying out the batt (fibres)
b) Wetting and setting the batt
c) Hardening
d) Milling or fulling

Laying out the batt :
1. Lay out towel on flat firm surface. Make sure that towel does not hang down over the edge of work surface.
2. Place bamboo mat on the towel.
3. Pull out small sections of white merino tops 8-10cm in length and place in a line 60cm in length along one edge of the mat.
4. Place a second line of fibre pieces on the mat, half overlapping the first line like tiles on a roof. Continue in this way until the required area of 60 x 60 cm has been covered.

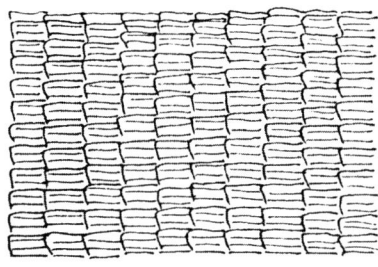
layer 1

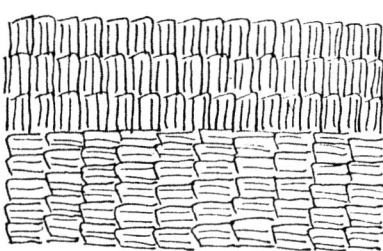
layer 2

5. Place a second layer of fibres on top of the first layer at right angles to it (see diagram).

Wetting and setting :
6. Make up felting solution by dissolving a small quantity of washing up liquid in one pint of boiling water. Pour this solution into the spray bottle and spray the fibres lightly with the solution. This helps to keep the fibres under control and begins the wetting out process.
7. Place a third layer of undyed fibre in position in the same direction as the first layer and spray with felting solution.
8. Place a fourth and final layer of coloured fibres in position and spray. Fibres in the top layer may be placed on at random and in whatever direction you wish to achieve for the pattern required. (When preparing a series of samples it is useful to try a variety of methods on the top layer to find the different effects which are possible).
9. Cover fibres carefully with the net, add more felting solution by pouring directly from the bottle (remove spray top) in the direction shown in diagram.

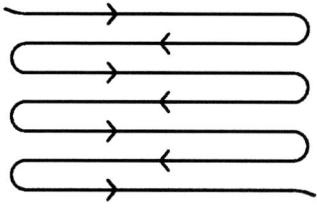

Carefully pat fibres with palm of hand until they are wet through. Make up more solution with detergent and very hot water as required. Using a circular motion and keeping the hands flat, gently rub the fibres with the net on top until they are wet through and there are no pockets of air between them. If they start to pill up through the net then stop at once.
10. Remove the net gently. Lift the fibres carefully from the mat, turn them over and lay face downwards.
11. Cover with net, add more hot solution making sure that fibres are thoroughly wet and continue rubbing for one to two minutes.
12. Remove net and turn felt design side up.

Hardening :
13. Place broom handle on edge of felt which is nearest to you and roll the felt and the bamboo mat firmly around the broom handle. Roll backwards and forwards on the work surface for five to ten minutes pressing firmly down on the felt. Open up the roll, stretch out the felt to ensure that there are no creases, give it a quarter turn and reroll. Pour some hot water over the rolled up felt and continue rolling for another five to ten minutes. After the second rolling turn the felt over before giving a quarter turn and rerolling - this time roll without the dowel for five minutes. Repeat the turning for a fourth time again without the dowel and roll for five minutes so that the felt has been rolled from every direction and on both sides, twice with the dowel in place and twice using only the mat.
14. Test the piece to see if the fibres are firmly felted. To do this try to pick up a few fibres between finger and thumb - if felting is complete they will not lift from the surface. A second method for testing is to take hold of one corner of the felt and move it between thumb and fingers - there should be no movement between the layers of fibres.
15. To complete the felting process it must now be milled.

Milling :
During this milling the felt will shrink in the direction of rolling, so it is important to check the size after each rolling and also to change the direction of rolling each time.
1. Unroll felt and remove from bamboo mat. Measure felt and make a note of dimensions.
2. Lay out piece of cotton cloth which should be larger all round than felt.
3. Lay felt on cotton, fold edges of cotton over felt and roll felt up tightly in the cloth.

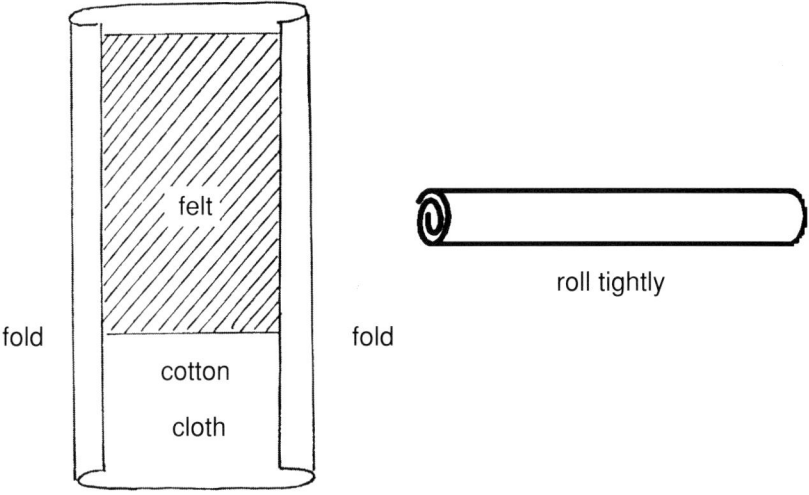

4. Place rolled up felt in gravel tray or in sink and pour boiling water over. Wearing rubber gloves to avoid scalding, remove felt from tray and roll backwards and forwards on a firm surface for one minute only. A ribbed surface such as a draining board or felting board will speed up the milling process
5. Open rolled felt after one minute, measure, give a quarter turn and reroll.
6. Repeat this process until the required degree of milling is obtained, this will be determined by the intended use. Felt for embroidery will not require as much milling as felt for clothing.
7. Rinse out all soap, spin dry, pull into shape and press firmly with a hot iron while still damp. Lay flat to dry.

Dealing with the edges when making a flat piece of felt
If the completed piece of felt is to be cut up and seamed, then the edges can be ignored during the felting process, but if the finished edges are to be seen, as in the case of a decorative wallhanging, then it is necessary to deal with them throughout the process of making the felt.

After the fibres have been wetted out and rubbed to flatten them, there are three possible ways of dealing with the edges :
(a) fold under any straggling ends of fibre.
(b) trim the edges to the required shape.

When the bamboo mat is opened after each rolling, the edges should be checked and either knocked back into shape or trimmed when necessary. Trimming and knocking into shape should be done in the early stages of hardening so that the edges are well set before milling begins.

(c) A third method is particularly useful when using fleece. Before the batt is wetted, a small quantity of teased wool is inserted between two layers all around the edges. This helps to prevent spreading and thinning. As previously described, the edges should be checked and knocked into shape during the hardening process.

Surface Design

Laying Coloured Fibres on the Surface

Different effects can be achieved by the methods used in applying the coloured fibres to the surface of the felt.

1. To achieve a blended effect, the coloured fibres should be thoroughly mixed before they are applied. This is most easily done using carders but can be done by hand if the fibres are teased out carefully and colours combined before they are applied.

How to use hand carders to blend coloured fibres:

(a) Place the coloured fibres to be blended on the left-hand carder in the the proportions required.
(b) Lightly draw the other carder over the fibres, repeating this action until the colours begin to blend.
(d) Transfer all the fibres to the right-hand carder and repeat the brushing action until the required degree of colour blending is achieved
(e) Loosen the fibres from the carders by placing the lower edge of one carder on the lower edge of the other and brushing upwards so that the fibres are lifted free of the metal teeth.
(f) Remove the fibres which are now ready for use.

2. Coloured fibres can be applied to the surface of the base batt by pulling them out from a combed top in the same way as the base was laid down. The fibres will shrink back along their own length, making interesting ripples - this can be useful if a directional emphasis is required in the design.

3. A textured effect can be obtained by chopping up the fibres, mixing the colours and applying to the surface. The many short ends created by the chopping ensure good felting but the effect is not as smooth as that achieved by blending the fibres.

(a)
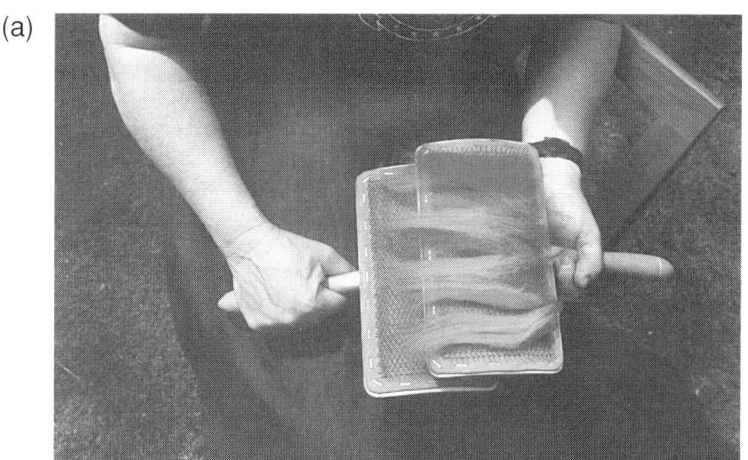

(b)
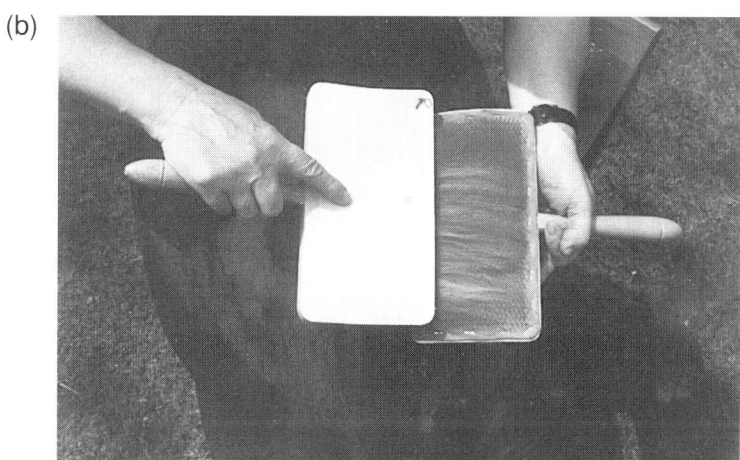

(c)
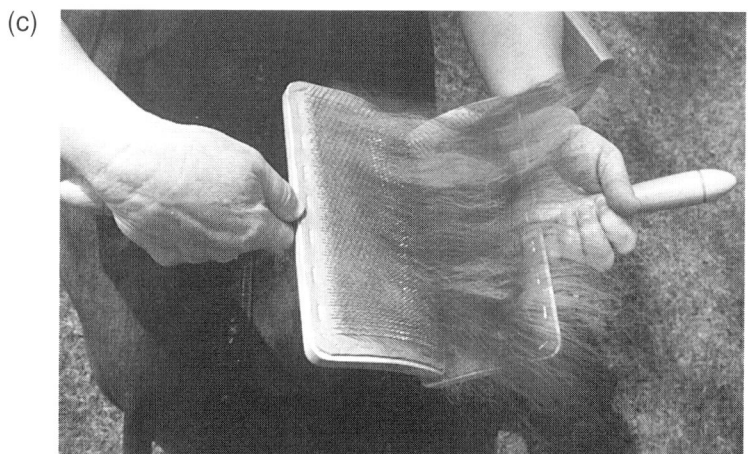

Blending coloured fibres with hand carders

Further Techniques

Once the basic technique of making a piece of felt has been mastered there are many ways in which individual designs can be created. If the design calls for clear shapes which retain their definition throughout the felting process then 'half-felt' is required. As its name suggests 'half-felt' describes fibres which have been treated just enough to enable them to hold together in a sheet but which have not begun to shrink and felt. It is useful to build up a selection of 'half-felts' in different colours so that they are ready to use as required.

To make 'half-felt'
1. Lay out two layers of fibres on bamboo mat (see instructions for making basic felt)
2. Spray fibres with detergent solution.
3. Cover with net, add enough detergent solution to wet through.
4. Rub gently with palm of hand to remove all air bubbles.
5. Gently remove the net.
6. Roll firmly in bamboo mat with a dowel for 5 minutes.
7. Open up the roll, turn the fibres over and reroll for 5 minutes.
8. Test with fingers to see if fibres are holding together but not felting.
9. Rinse very carefully and gently squeeze out water.
10. Iron on both sides and lay out flat to dry.

Inlay Technique
In this technique the shapes to be inlaid are cut out of prepared 'half-felted' pieces. The background batt of fibres is laid down in the usual way, covered with net, wetted out and rubbed lightly just enough to flatten the fibres. The net is then removed. The cut pieces of 'half-felt' which are to form the pattern are carefully laid on the surface of the background batt and pressed down so that they adhere to the wet fibres below. If it is crucial that the pattern pieces do not move at all then they should be lightly tacked in position with fairly large tacking stitches.

The net is then replaced and the inlaid pieces gently rubbed to ensure that they are thoroughly wetted. The net is removed and the felting process continued. After the two rollings with the dowel in place any tacking stitches should be removed to prevent them becoming enmeshed in the felt.

As the fibres begin to felt the 'half-felted' shapes become an integral part of the main piece. A good way to test this is to make a sample with brightly coloured 'half-felted' pieces on a light coloured background. When the felting is complete the coloured outlines of the inlaid shapes are clearly visible on the underside of the felt, showing that the coloured fibres are thoroughly felted in with the background fibres and not just sitting on the surface.

Mosaic Technique

Another method of using 'half-felt' builds up a pattern by fitting pieces carefully together over the whole surface of the felt like a mosaic. Using this method the surface of the felt is completely level unlike the inlay technique where the inlaid pieces are slightly above the level of the background fibres.

To make a mosaic pattern two layers of different coloured 'half felt' are put one on top of the other. A paper pattern is then pinned in position through both layers and the required shape carefully cut out. When cutting out the shapes the point of the scissors should be inserted as close as possible to the edge of the pattern so that the felt surrounding the pattern remains intact. If a dark and a light colour are used the dark shape cut from the dark felt can be inserted in the identical space left in the light felt and vice versa. To keep the pieces in place they should be lightly tacked with fairly long oversewing stitches. Once the mosaic pattern has been built up it should be placed on to a background batt of unfelted fibres and the whole package then felted together. When the fibres begin to hold together carefully remove the tacking stitches before completing the felting processes.

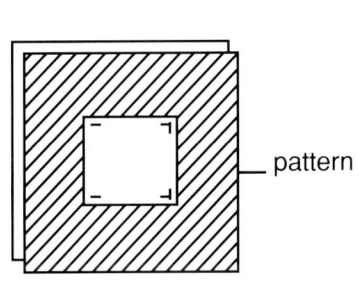

pattern

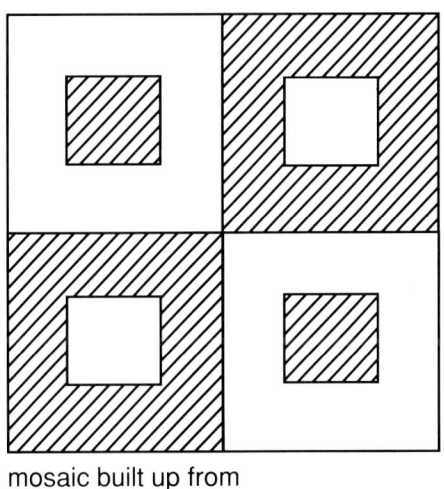

mosaic built up from light and dark felt

Weaving 'half-felt'

A third way in which 'half-felt' can be used is to cut it into strips and weave it together to form a pattern. By using different colours, different interlacings and if wished, different widths of strips, interesting designs can be formed. Once the strips have been interwoven the piece should be tacked together around the edges to hold them in place and the whole piece laid onto a batt of unfelted fibres and felted together. Again the tacking stitches should be removed before they become enmeshed in the felt. If the piece being 'woven' is large then it is helpful to pin the top of each vertical strip down on to a piece of soft fibre board and then as each horizontal strip is woven in, it should be pushed up into position and each end pinned before tacking to hold it in place.

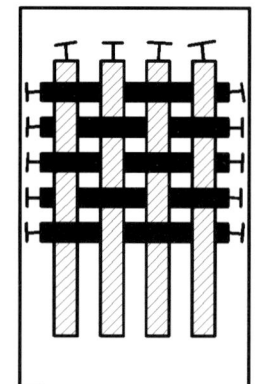

felt strips pinned on board

Multi-layered felt
This is built up from layers of different coloured fibre and may be made from unfelted fibres, 'half-felt' or a mixture of both. This can be time consuming to make as it takes time for the felting process to take place in the inner layers but is very effective. Once completed, parts of the top layers can be cut away to reveal the colours underneath. If the felt is left fairly soft the edges spring back when cut which can be very suitable for purely decorative purposes. If the felt is well hardened and milled, the edges remain firm after cutting.

Needled felt may be used for all inlay, mosaic, woven and layered techniques. The way in which needled felt is made causes the fibres to hold together in a web but as they are not subjected to moisture and heat they do not shrink. When used for any of the above techniques the needled felt is subjected to moisture, friction and heat and therefore the fibres shrink and felt in the same way as fibres used straight from combed tops.

Incorporating other fibres, yarns and fabrics into felt
Yarns and scraps of fabric can be added to the surface of the wool fibres before felting begins. This can produce interesting results. As the felting progresses, the wool fibres shrink, causing the yarns and fabric to wrinkle up and produce textured effects. Fibres with a hairy or textured surface, e.g. mohair or boucle yarns, work well and fabrics with a slightly rough surface adhere better than fabrics which are too smooth. To help fabric adhere to the surface of the felt it is a good idea to fray out some threads around the edges of the pieces before placing them on the wool fibres - the short ends of the threads then become caught up in the fibres.

Different effects can be obtained by laying the wool fibres on to a layer of fabric and felting both together. If the fabric is fairly loosely woven then this technique works particularly well. As the felting progresses some of the fibres make their way through the weave structure of the fabric and as they fibres shrink the material contracts producing a textured surface. The results achieved vary with the fabric used - cotton muslins and scrims work well giving a fine texture on the reverse of the felt while synthetic chiffons produce a more textured bubbled effect. Open weave cottons can be first decorated by printing, painting or tie dyeing before laying on the wool fibres and as the felt shrinks so too does the pattern on the fabric and again interesting textures appear.

Using Silk with Felt
Wool felt has a matt surface and interesting effects can be achieved by the introduction of some lustrous silk fibres as a surface decoration. There are different ways in which this can be done :
a) by adding a layer of rainbow dyed Mawata silk cap to the surface of the wet felt batt before hardening begins. The result is a cobweb effect of colour and texture on the surface which works well over a whole piece. It is not necessary to use an even layer of silk as an uneven effect can add to the surface interest.
b) by adding a layer of silk cap to the surface of a half-felted batt. The half-felted pieces can then be cut into desired shapes and used as an inlay design.
d) silk fibres can be made into paper-like sheets which can be cut up and added to the surface of the felt batt.

Method A
1. Lay out wool fibre batt, cover with net, wet through and rub to flatten.
2. Pull one layer of silk from the cap and stretch out to the thickness required.
3. Lay silk on to wet wool batt and press into place. Silk is often difficult to wet through and it may be necessary to add extra detergent solution to make it adhere to the surface of the wool. A potato masher is a useful tool for this.
4. Cover with net and rub gently until the silk begins to adhere to the wool.
5. Remove net and continue to felt in the usual way.

Method B
1. Silk cap should be added to the surface of a half-felted batt as in method A.
2. Only carry out the felting process enough to make the wool fibres hold on to the silk. This can then be cut into shapes and used for inlay.

Method C
1. Lay out several sheets of newspaper on top of each other.
2. Place a piece of mosquito netting (obtainable from camping equipment suppliers) on the newspaper.
3. Make up wallpaper paste to a fairly runny consistency. (If possible use a paste without fungicide but if this is difficult to obtain, wear rubber gloves and wash hands immediately after use).
4. Either lay out one layer of silk taken from a silk cap and then lay a second layer on top or lay out a thin layer of silk fibres taken from a silk top in the same way as wool fibres are laid out for felting then lay a second thin layer of fibres on top at right angles to the first layer.
5. Cover the silk with a second piece of mosquito netting.

6. Using a sponge, work some wallpaper paste into the silk through the netting. Turn the package over and repeat from the other side.
7. Roll the package on both sides with a piece of dowelling to flatten and leave to dry.
8. When dry, carefully peel off the netting and the silk will be in a thin sheet ready for use.
9. The sheet of silk fibres can be cut up and added to the surface of wool. As the felt is made incorporating the silk pieces the water and detergent will wash away the wallpaper paste and leave the silk adhering to the surface of the felt.

Dyeing Silk

Silk fibres readily absorb dye and if dyed in a 'rainbow' or random fashion can greatly add interest to the surface of the felt. There are two simple methods of 'rainbow' dyeing silk:
a) steaming
b) using a microwave oven

The type of dyes used for this type of dyeing are known as acid dyes and are suitable for use on protein fibres such as silk and wool. These can be obtained from specialist suppliers or by mail order - see list of suppliers for details. The dyes are supplied in powder form but are easier to handle if made up into solution before use.

When using dyes at home, particularly in the kitchen, it is important to remember that they are chemical substances and to take certain safety precautions:

1. Remove all cooking utensils from the area to be used.
2. Protect the work surface with newspaper and a layer of plastic.
3. Wear rubber gloves when handling dyes.
4. Do not breath in dye powder - wear a mask if you are using the dye powders frequently.
5. Store dyes in clearly labelled containers, in a cool dark place and well out of the reach of children.
6. All utensils used for dyeing should be kept for that purpose and should not be stored beside cooking utensils. Small beakers, glass stirring rods and plastic syringes can be purchased from specialist suppliers.

To make dye powder into solution:
1. Weigh out 1g of dye powder into a beaker or small container. (If you do not have scales to measure this small quantity use 1 teaspoonful dye powder instead).
2. Add a small quantity of hot water and stir until the dye powder is dissolved.
3. Add boiling water to the beaker and make up solution to 100ml. Stir and allow to cool. (If you do not have a measuring beaker just add approximately 100ml of boiling water.

4. When cool this solution can be stored until required in a sealed and clearly labelled bottle - and will keep for several months.

Preparing the silk cap or fibre to be dyed:
Silk fibres can be difficult to wet through and as the dyes will be applied to wet fibres it is advisable to soak the silk for several hours or preferably overnight before dyeing. Fill a large bowl with warm water, add a few drops of washing up liquid and half a cupful of white vinegar and place the silk in the bowl. If the silk tends to rise to the surface place a plate on top to keep the silk submerged.

How to Dye the silk:
1. Lay out a pad of newspaper larger than the cap or fibre to be dyed.
2. Lay a piece of plastic on top of the paper again larger than the fibre to be dyed (a large freezer bag slit down one side and along the lower edge and opened out flat is ideal).
3. Squeeze the silk gently from the soaking solution removing any excess water.
4. Lay the silk on the plastic and open it out flat.
5. Choose one colour of dye solution and place in a syringe or small container.
6. Apply the dye to one area of the silk either in spots, lines or zigzags. Continue until you have applied as much of the first colour as you wish.
7. Choose the second colour of dye and apply in the same way. Allow some of this colour to overlap the first colour so that the colours mix.
8. Repeat with a third colour if you wish.
9. Gently press down on the silk with gloved hands or use flat bottom of a container. (A potato masher kept for this purpose is ideal). Press the dye solutions into the silk - there should just be no excess dye.
10. Carefully turn the silk over and check the underside; add more dye in the same way if there are any undyed areas and press into the silk.
11. Fold the plastic over the silk to form a small flat package.
12. Place the package in a steamer or metal colander over a pan of boiling water, cover and steam for one hour to set the dyes.
13. Remove package from steamer, allow to cool and then rinse carefully in warm water until water runs clear.
14. Squeeze out excess water and leave to dry.

If you have a microwave available:
Follow the above instructions to the end of stage 10.

Place the silk in a container suitable for use in a microwave and seal carefully with cling film. Microwave on full power for five minutes, allow to stand for two or three minutes and then microwave again on half power for a further five minutes. Allow to cool and rinse and dry as above.

Using fabric paints and dyes
Designs can be painted on the surface of the already made felt - this may be done using fabric paints or certain kinds of dye, e.g. 'Coolwool'. Stencilling is a very satisfactory method of applying paint or dye as it is possible to work the colour well into the felt. Felt can be tie dyed after it is made or random dyed in a flat tray using dyes in powder form - it is best to follow the suppliers' instructions.

Patchwork
Patterns can be created by invisibly stitching small pieces of felt together - this is an ideal way in which to use up scraps left over from other projects.

Quilting
Hand or machine-stitching can be used to decorate and to reinforce felt especially if spirals or zigzag lines are used. This technique of stitching on felt is apparent on many ethnic examples.

Embroidery
Embroidery is a very useful addition to the surface of felt. It may be done by hand or machine. Surface stitching adds interest as it creates contours and breaks up the otherwise flat surface of the felt.

Interesting textures created by felting on to different fabrics

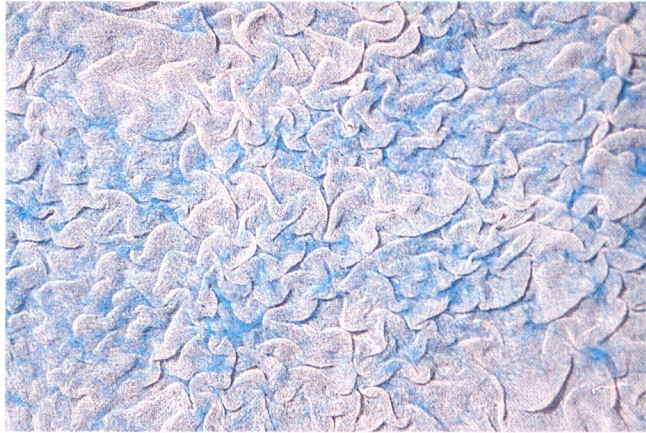

(a) Polyester georgette

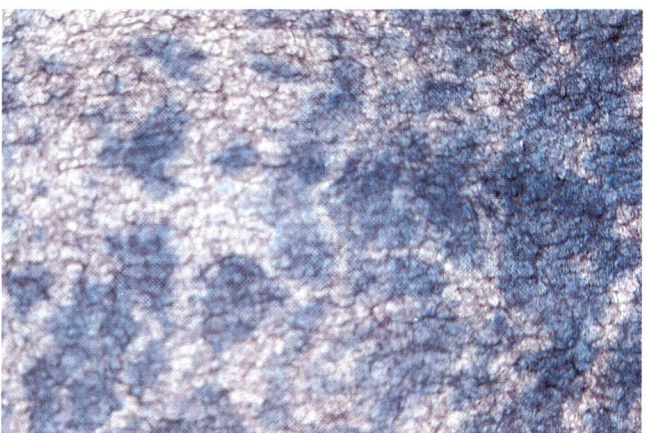

(b) tie-dyed muslin

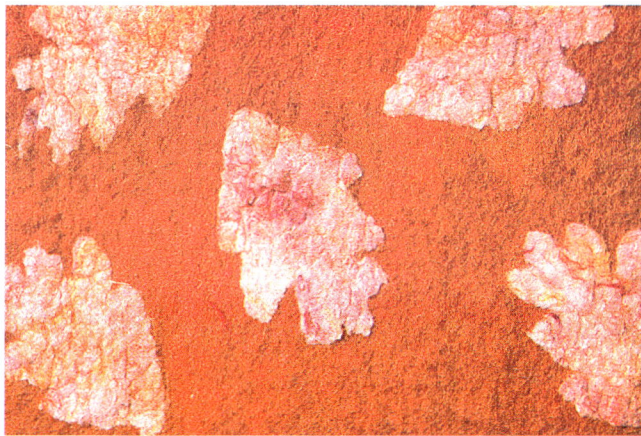

(c) 'silk paper' leaves

Felts from natural fleeces

(a) White Faced Woodland felt embroidered with handspun wool and silk yarns

(b) Hanging composed of panels of twenty two different fleece types. Size: 100cm x 40cm

(a) 'Dry Stone Wall'
Hanging made from a selection of natural coloured fleeces

(b) Kendal Castle
Hanging - size 150cm x 200cm

(a) Waistcoat - merino fibre felted on to a muslin backing to give lightweight but strong fabric. Decorated with rainbow dyed silk fibres

(b) Collection of hats

Three-Dimensional Felt

So far all the techniques covered have been incorporated into felt produced as a flat piece but it is also possible to make it in a three dimensional seamless form. This method of production is used extensively by Scandinavian feltmakers for hats, bags, mittens and boots. The success of this technique depends on confident handling of the fibres and calls for rather more skill than is required for the flat method so it is advisable for the feltmaker to have some experience before tackling this method.

Bags are an ideal first project for three dimensional feltmaking and can be made in a wide variety of shapes and sizes. For a first time avoid a shape which is too small and fiddly and avoid being over ambitious and tackling a shape which is too large. A good size to begin with would be approximately 24 cm wide and 20 cm high with a 10 cm flap. *See diagrams for instructions for making the template.*

Making the pattern for a seamless bag:
1. First decide on the shape and size of the bag to be made. Cut this shape in paper to check that the size is correct.
2. Add 40% to the measurements of both length and width to allow for shrinkage.
3. Once the final measurements have been calculated a template should be cut to this size.

Some simple shapes for bags suitable for first projects.

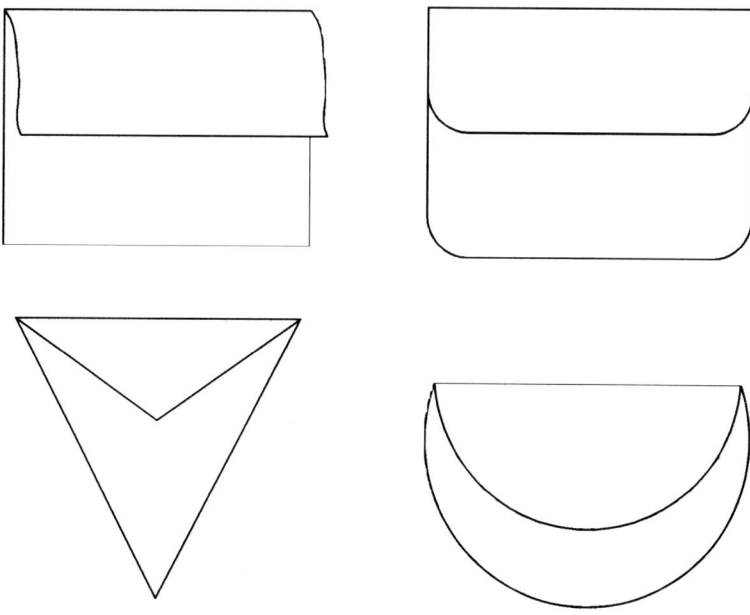

Making Templates

Templates may be made from cardboard, cloth or plastic. If using cardboard, firm packing cartons are ideal and after cutting the template the edges can be reinforced by covering with sticky parcel-tape. Avoid using card which has a decorative surface such as mounting board as this surface will transfer itself to the wool fibres during felting. If cloth is chosen it needs to be firm and closely woven. It is easy to wet out the fibres using a cloth template but it can adhere to the fibres during felting unless great care is taken. Plastic templates are easier to use if the plastic is of a heavy weight as the edges can be followed when building up the shape and such templates also have the advantage of being reuseable. The plastic used by builders for laying under concrete is ideal and heavy weights of plastic sheeting can also be purchased at garden centres.

How to make a template for a bag finished size 24cm x 20 cm
(allowing 40% for shrinkage)

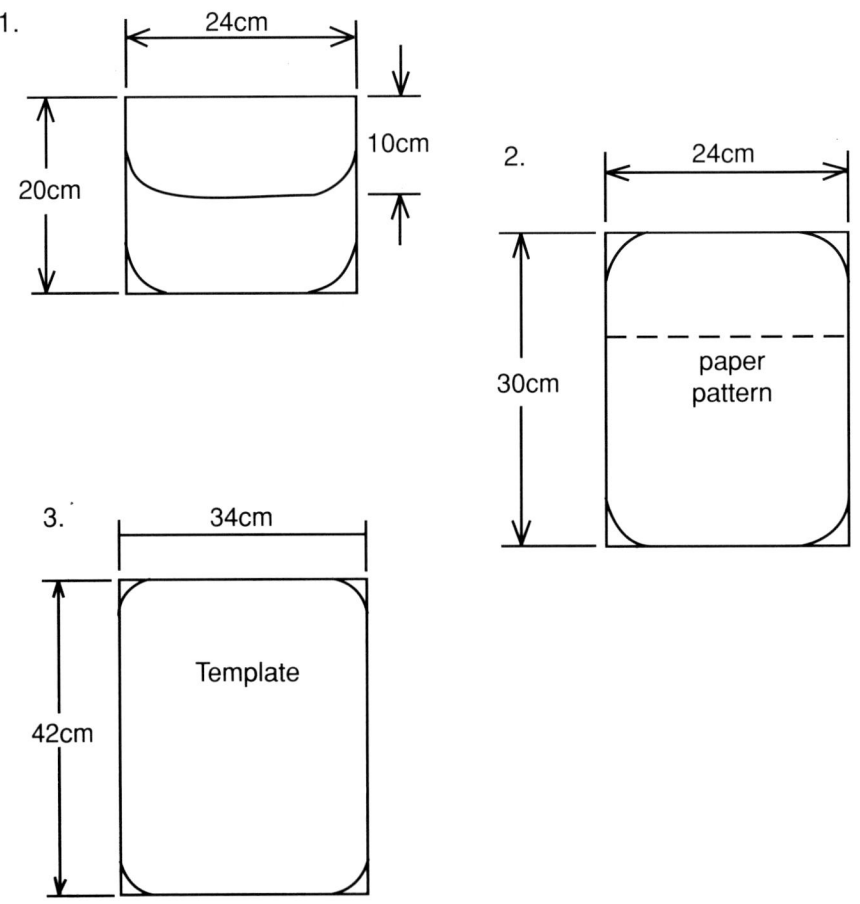

To make a simple three-dimensional felt bag

1. Lay out folded towel with bamboo blind on top.
2. Lay plastic template on bamboo mat.
3. Pull out small lengths of combed tops and lay these pieces around the edge with half the length overlapping the edge of the template as in *diagram (a)*
4. Continue to pull out lengths of fibre in this way and fill in the shape of the pattern with overlapping layers in the same way as you would for a flat piece *see diagram (b)*
5. Place a second layer of overlapping fibres at right angles to the first one but this time the fibres should only reach the edge of the template *see diagram (c)*

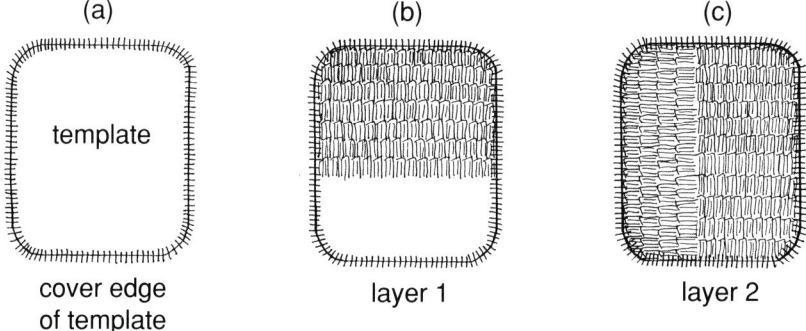

6. *Carefully* pour hot water with some detergent in to the centre of the fibres taking care not to disturb the layers. Gently press the fibres so that the water is absorbed and work from the centre outwards but do not allow the edges of the fibres which overlap the template to get wet.
7. *Carefully* lift the template and fibres and turn over so that the template is on top.
8. Turn the overlapping fibres back over the edge of the template *see diagram (d)*
9. Put one layer of overlapping fibres on top of the template until it is covered, this layer should lie in the same direction as the first layer of side one *see diagram (e)*
10. Lay a second layer of overlapping fibres at right angles to the first layer allowing the fibres to overlap the template *see diagram (f)*

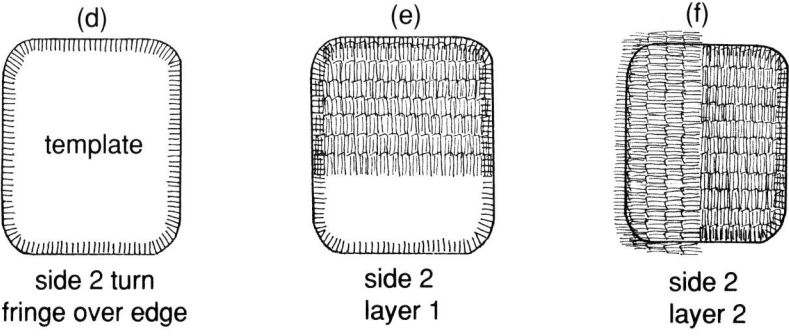

11. Wet these fibres and press the water through until all layers are wet.
12. Turn fibres and template over, turn the overlapping fibres back over the edge so that the resulting package is the same size as the template.
13. Add a third layer of overlapping fibres at right angles to the last one and wet.
14. Turn package and fold over any overlapping edges.
15. Add third layer of fibre to the second side, wet and tuck in any edges.
16. Cover fibres with net and gently rub over the surface, rubbing from the edges inwards to keep the package exactly the size of the template, stop when fibres start to come through the net.
17. Turn package over, cover with net and repeat the rubbing process.
18. Remove net and add any decoration rubbing gently to get it to adhere to the wool fibres.
19. Gently roll the package up in the bamboo blind using a dowell to keep it flat.
20. Roll gently for two to three minutes, open up, turn package over and repeat.
21. Continue in this way until the fibres begin to harden but take care not to form a hard seam around the edge.
22. When fibres have hardened sufficiently to handle or the template begins to curl carefully cut the fibres along the bottom of the package and remove the plastic template *see diagram (g)*.
23. Reroll in mat for two to three minutes, open up to ensure that the two sides of the bag are not felting together. turn over and repeat.

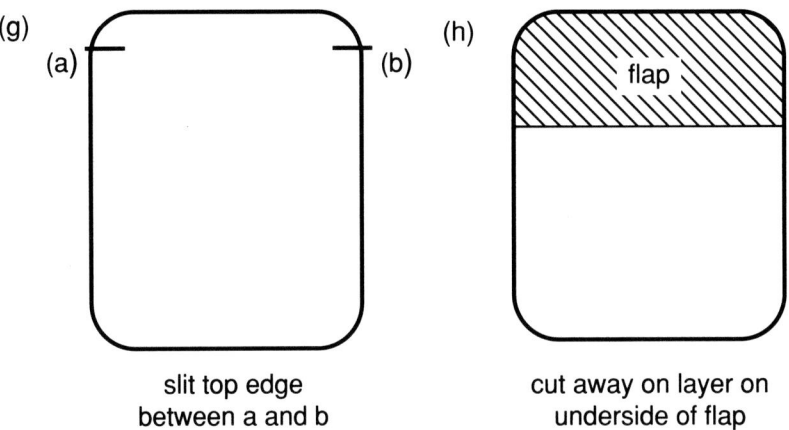

(g) slit top edge between a and b

(h) cut away on layer on underside of flap

Hardening is continued in this way, gradually adding more hot water and increasing the pressure. The bag must be turned inside out so that hardening can be carried out on the inside. When the bag is hardening satisfactorily remove dowel and roll only in the mat.

At this point the felt should be cut away from the underside of the flap so that the flap edges will become satisfactorily felted *see diagram (h)*. Hold up to the light and see if there are any weak or thin places - these should be rubbed by hand to shrink and strengthen them. Test the felt between finger and thumb, checking for any movement between the layers of the fibres (See basic sampling instructions). When hardening is complete the bag should then be milled in the same way as a flat piece of felt. Rinse the bag and spin out excess water. Pull into shape and iron, then leave to dry.

Decoration:
The felt package may be decorated by any of the following methods :
Wisps of coloured tops
Cut out half-felted pieces
Fancy yarns
Dyed silk
Any decoration is best added to the outside after step 17.

Making Felt Cones and Capelines for Hatmaking

Felt cones are used to make small fairly close fitting hats such as pillbox styles which are worn on the back of the head or tilted forward over the brow, and cloches which fit closely to the head and come down over the ears.

Capelines are larger and used to make hats with brims.

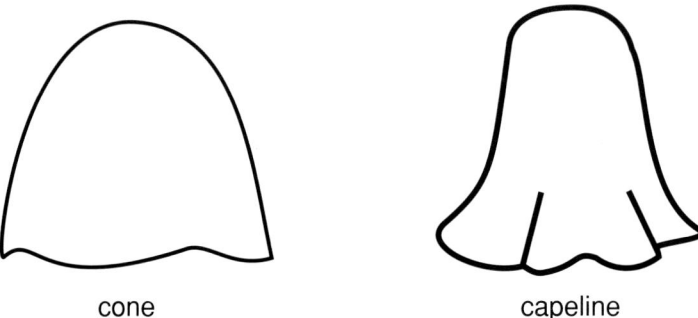

cone   capeline

The basic shape from which all the other patterns can be developed is the cone shape.

To make a pattern for a felt cone you require two measurements:
a)   the measurement around the head taken just above the eyebrows and the tops of the ears.
b)   the measurement over the top of the head to half way down each ear.

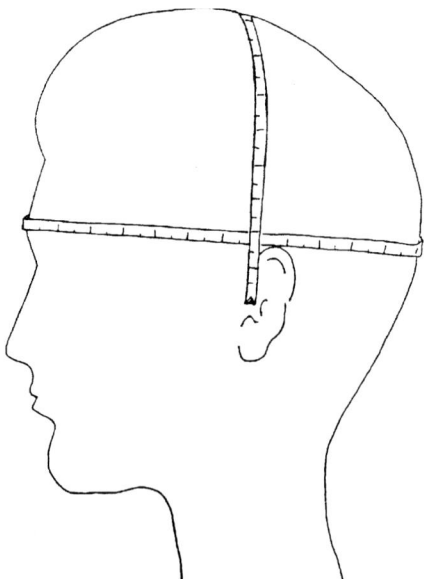

Once you have taken these measurements divide each in half and add 40% for shrinkage.

example: Measurement (a) = $\frac{56cm}{2}$ = 28cm $\frac{28 \times 4}{10}$ = 11.2

28 + 11.2 = 39.2   *say 40 cm*

Measurement (b) = $\frac{36cm}{2}$ = 18cm $\frac{18 \times 4}{10}$ = 7.2 cm

18 + 7.2 = 25.2   *say 25 cm*

Use these measurements to draw a rectangle with (a) as the width and (b) as the height.
Mark in the centre point of the top line.
Draw in a curve for the crown of the hat by joining the lower corners of the rectangle with the centre top point - make sure this curve is not too shallow.
The basic rectangle can then be adapted to make the required shape for the different types of hat. *See diagrams below:*

Hat with brim

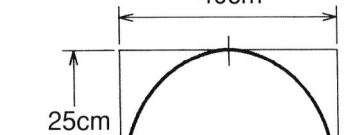

Cloche

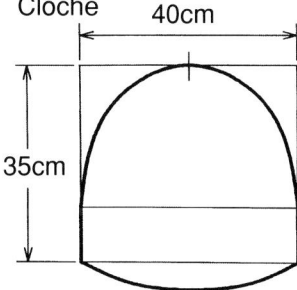

Rolled brim

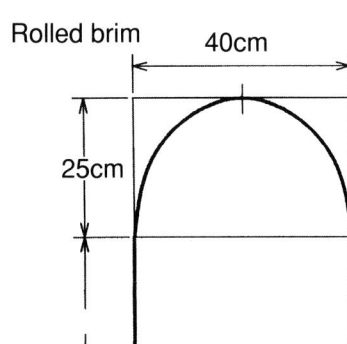

Pointed cone

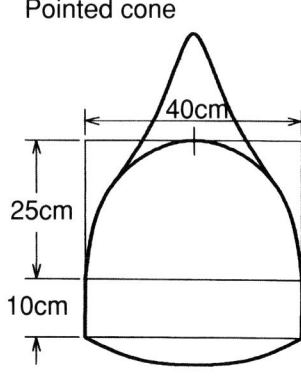

U-Shaped Hoods
A U-shaped hood is the same width all the way down but is much deeper than the cone. The extra depth is to allow for rolling up or folding the lower edge or to make a hood-shaped hat which comes right down to or below the level of the chin.

To make a rolled edge: Stretch the hood on a hat block taking care not to stretch the lower edge. Begin by rolling up a small section of the edge and pin in position. Repeat this process with the next section of the edge and pin this in position; continue in this way until the whole of the edge is rolled. The pins can then be removed and the hood left on the block to dry.

To make the felt cone
Once the shape and size has been calculated a paper pattern should then be made for the required size of cone. A template is cut in the same way as for the felt bag. But note that this time the pattern already includes the allowance for shrinkage so the template should be cut to the same size as the paper pattern.

To make the felt cone follow steps 1 - 22 of the method and instructions given for the bag. The main difference between making the cone and the bag is that it is important that the cone is kept even all the way around, and that attention is paid to avoiding thick ridges or weak spots which could cause problems when blocking the hat *(see also photographs on pages 44 and 45)*.

To avoid ridges: place one hand inside the cone to support it and using a little detergent on the other hand to act as a lubricant carefully rub along the line where the fibres were folded over the edge of the template. If there is any sign of a ridge turn the cone carefully wrong side out and repeat the rubbing process.

To check for thin places: hold cone up to the light and if any thin places are visible they should be treated to the rubbing treatment which shrinks the fibres and consequently the thin areas. Once any necessary 'First Aid' treatment has been administered then the hardening can be continued as for the bag but each time the cone is unfolded it should be rerolled with a different part at the edge to avoid forming a ridge.

If the lower edges of the cone begin to stretch out of shape with the rolling it is possible to shrink them by rolling only the lower part of the cone in the mat and continuing the felting process.

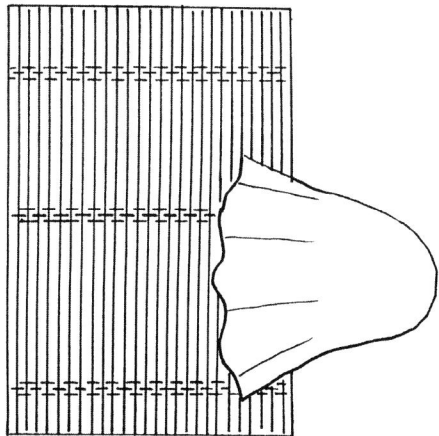

When the cone is hardened and milled *(see instructions for three-dimensional bags)* it is ready for shaping and blocking.

To block a felt cone
1. First cover the hat block to be used with clingfilm. This will prevent the possible transference of dye from any previous hat.
2. Steam the felt cone by holding it over the spout of a boiling kettle. This will make the felt more elastic and will help it to stretch more easily.
3. Place the cone on to the hat block and firmly ease and stretch it downwards until it fits the block. If there is any fullness at the crown of the block this can be eased away by resteaming the felt while on the block, and knocking the steam back into the felt using the side of the hand or by hammering the felt lightly with a rolling pin or wooden hammer. Pressing with a steam iron and damp cloth can also help remove unwanted fullness.
4. When the cone is stretched satisfactorily then hold in place with a piece of cord held with a slip knot; a piece of elastic or by pinning to the block with drawing-pins which will not rust. The depth of crown should be taken into consideration and the ties or drawing-pins should be just below the required depth. If the hat is to have a turned up brim it is useful to place something around the lower edge of the blocked crown so that the brim can be turned up over this while it dries. A padded roll can be made from cotton cloth bound with string or from plastic foam pipe-lagging which can be shaped to the right size and held in position with masking tape. Either of these methods will help to shape the brim and while it dries it will develop a curve rather than a fold.
6. When dry the hat may be left soft and unstiffened but if the design is a more formal one it is better to stiffen so that it will hold its shape *(see photographs on page 46)*.

(a)
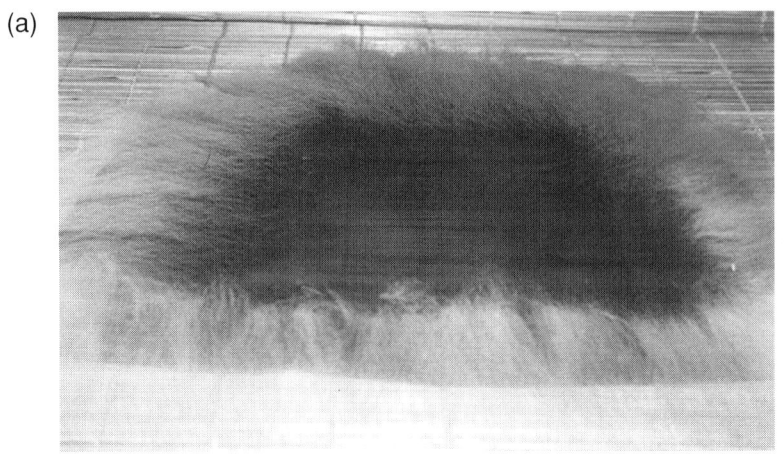

(b)

(c)
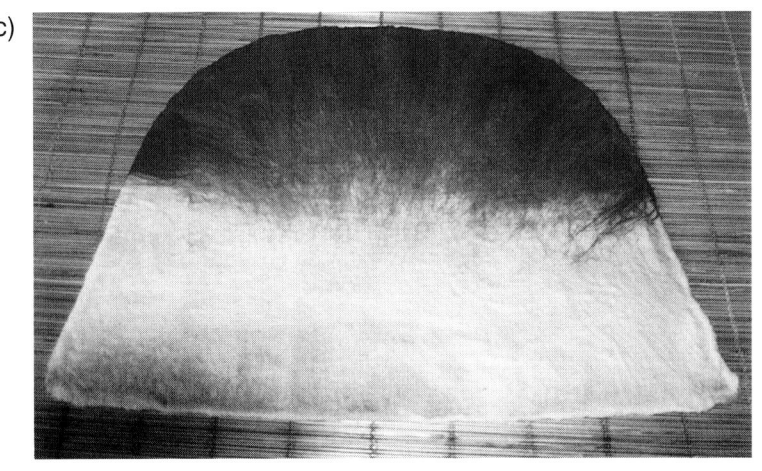

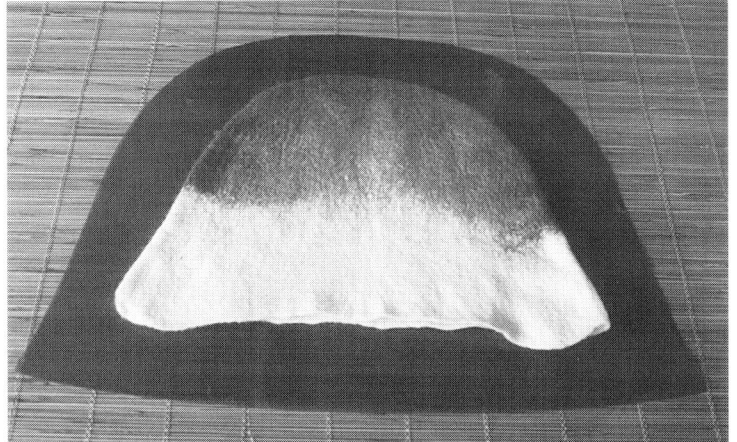

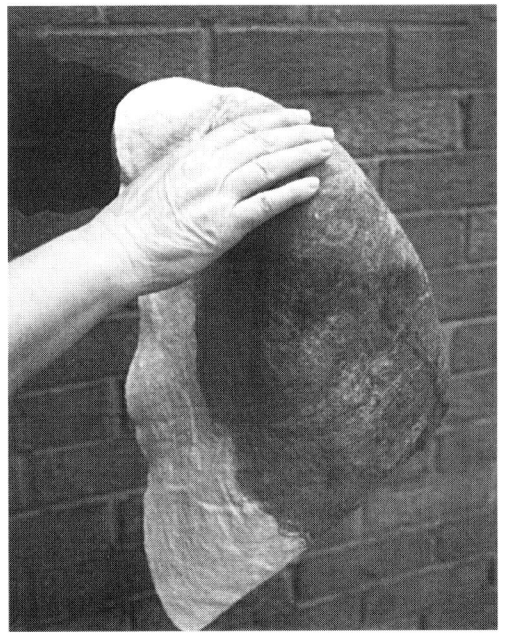

(a) Template with one layer of fibres around the edge
(b) Layer of fibres covering template completely
(c) Hood ready for felting
(d) Part felted hood on template illustrating the shrinkage which has taken place
(e) Rubbing to ensure that there are no thin places

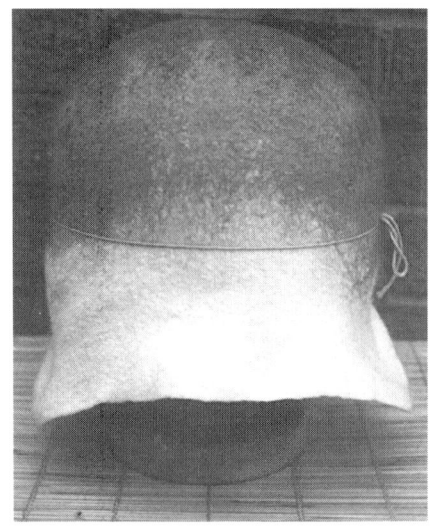
(a)

(b)

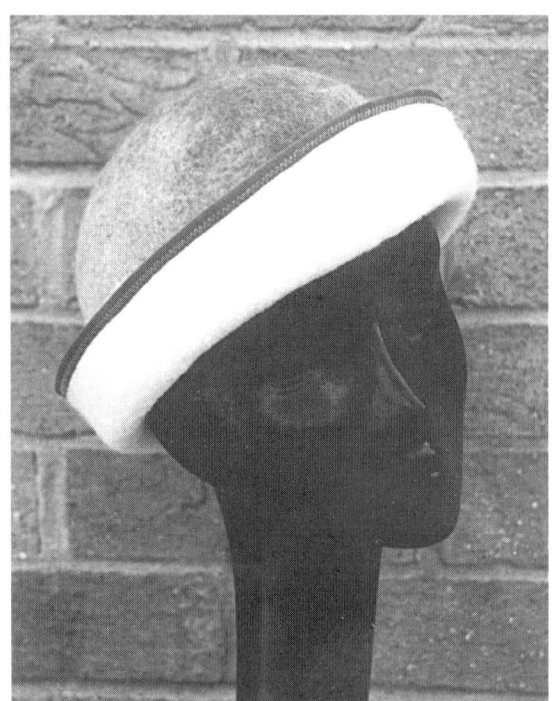
(c)

(a) Hood stretched and tied on hat block
(b) Brim turned back over plastic foam to shape it
(c) Completed hat

Hat blocks

These are made from hardwood in different shapes and head sizes. The felt hood is steamed, stretched and dried on the block so that it takes its size and shape from the one being used. These blocks are hand made by specialist makers and are consequently expensive. The amateur hat maker can try blocking over a pudding bowl or other household container large enough for their head.

Felt Stiffener

There are two types of stiffener available on the market, one is a solvent which is applied to the inside of dry felt and the other a water-based solution which can be applied to the wet felt.

The solvent is applied as a light coating with a brush and allowed to dry. Great care must be taken when using solvent. It should be used sparingly and applied in a well ventilated area. The water-based stiffener can also be applied with a brush or a spray but the most satisfactory method is to dilute the stiffener using one part stiffener to three parts water and immerse the wet felt in the solution. Squeeze out as much of the solution as possible, spin dry and then block the hat as usual. The diluted stiffener can be rebottled and used several times.

Making up the hat

Once the hat is blocked and dry it may be completed. The edge of the brim will need to be trimmed and finished off. If the hat is stiffened it is usual to wire the edge of the brim to hold it in shape. A headband made from petersham ribbon should also be stitched into the inside of the hat.

To wire a brim

Special millinery wire (see suppliers appendix) is used for this. It is available in different weights but the most frequently used size is no 6. The wire comes in a roll and must have excess spring removed from it before it is attached to the brim. To do this, first measure the length of wire required, cut off the length with wire cutters and then pull the wire through between thumb and forefinger while holding firmly and pulling against the curve.

A bound edge

1. Measure wire to fit the circumference of the brim plus approximately 5cm for overlap.
2. Shape the wire into a circle and hold the overlap temporarily in position with a little fuse wire.
3. Stitch the wire to the edge of the brim with strong cotton and using wire stitch. Start stitching at the back of the hat just to the left of the join in the wire. Adjust the wire to fit the brim exactly and oversew the overlapping ends.
4. After wiring the edge can be bound with petersham ribbon.

A turned edge

If the edge of the brim is to be turned under instead of bound then the wire should be stitched to the underside of the brim about 1cm in from the edge. After wiring, the edge of the brim can be folded under, pressed and machine stitched in position close to the edge of the wire. Finally any excess felt can be trimmed away close to the machine stitching.

Wire Stitch

Begin by firmly oversewing the wire to the edge of the brim two or three times. Working from right to left pass the thread over the wire and insert needle from back to front just under the wire and through the edge of the felt; pull the needle through and leave a loop of thread. Insert needle through the loop from the back to the front and pull thread up tight - this forms a small knot which lies on top of the wire and prevents the stitch from slipping. Repeat this around the brim. Stitches should be 13-19mm apart (1/2 - 3/4 inch).

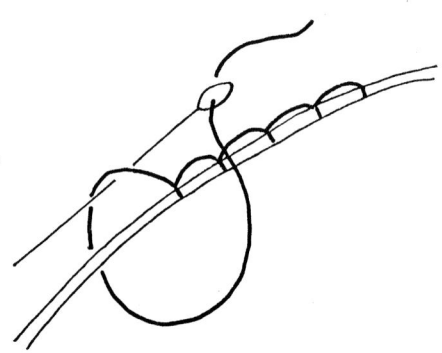

Headbands
A headband is a piece of petersham ribbon which is made to fit the size of the head and stitched into the inside of the lower edge of the crown. Cut off the required length of petersham ribbon which should be the head measurement plus 25mm for turnings. Steam press the ribbon and shape it into an arc by stretching one edge. Back stitch the two ends of the ribbon together and fit the headband into the hat with the larger edge to the lower edge of the crown and working from the centre back. Fix in position with pins inserted vertically and then stitch in place using stab stitch. If the hat is slightly larger than the headband it should be eased evenly onto the band to make it fit. Finally complete the hat by adding the trimming to the outside.

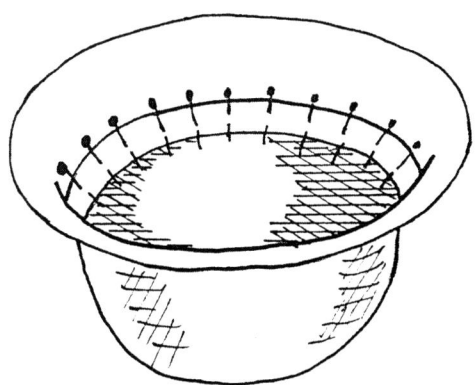

Felt for Garments

When producing felt which is intended for making up into garments there are several important factors which must be considered:
a)   the weight of the felt - is the garment for indoor or outdoor wear?
b)   style of the garment.
c)   will the garment be lined?
d)   the quantity of felt required.

The pattern - when buying a commercial pattern or designing your own pattern for felt garments it is best to stick to simple tailored shapes which are the most effective.

Estimating the size of felt needed - measure the length and width of pattern pieces and add 100% to the measurement in each direction to allow for shrinkage, e.g.

>   if a final measurement of 50cm is required:
>   final size 50cm add 50cm = 100cm.
>   50% shrinkage = 50cm

Making the felt - it is often easier to make the felt in two or more pieces rather than trying to make one very large piece because of the time, space and physical energy required. When making a waistcoat the felt for the fronts can be made in one piece and the felt for the back as a second piece. If this method is adopted it is essential to keep careful records so that the different pieces will match in weight and thickness. The weight of fibre required will vary from feltmaker to feltmaker also according to the thickness of felt required. A very rough guide would be to allow 300 - 500g for a waistcoat.

Keeping records - in order to produce two matching pieces of felt it is important to keep detailed records of fibres, measurements and methods used. The record sheet which appears in the section on record keeping is ideal for this. Divide the fibre in half and using one of these halves lay out the fibres for the first piece. Weigh any which are left so that the exact weight used can be calculated. Record this on the record sheet and use exactly the same weight when making the second half.

Using muslin as a backing - it can be useful to felt on to a layer of lightweight muslin when felting for garments as this enables a stable felt to be made using the minimum of fibre which keeps down the weight of the garment. If it is to be lined then the muslin backing will be hidden but if an unlined garment is required then the muslin can be decorated by tie-dyeing or printing before use which produces a very attractive effect.

Testing Fleece for Feltability

Although sheep breeds are classified according to their characteristics and quality, they can vary within each breed and each fleece can be further graded as explained in the chapter 'Fibres and Feltability'. Bearing in mind all these variations, the feltmaker should always make a sample of the selected fleece to ensure that the result is suitable for the purpose for which the felt is required. The test piece will also enable you to calculate the amount of fleece required for the project. See 'Record Keeping' and 'Sample Record Sheet'.

For the purposes of these tests the B.W.M.B. classification of sheep breeds was used for easy comparisons and standard reference.

Mountain and Hill	- 7 examples;	Longwool and Lustre	- 6 examples;
Shortwool and Down	- 8 examples;	Fine Wools	- 1 example;
Medium Type	- 4 examples;		

In all twenty six types of fleece were tested.

Method used for testing: A standard sample of scoured and carded fleece weighing 50g was used for each test. Each sample was laid out in four layers, wetted out, measured and then hardened for ten minutes by rubbing and rolling. The sample was then remeasured and one third was cut off and retained. The remaining two thirds of each sample was rolled until it was considered to be fully hardened and the time required to reach this stage was noted. The hardened sample was cut in half, one half being retained at that stage and the remaining piece was milled until no further shrinkage could be achieved. The milling time was noted and the sample was measured.

By comparing measurements at the start and finish, it was possible to establish the percentage of shrinkage for each sample and the time required to produce a fully felted piece, made it possible to compare the different felting rates.
The results are tabulated in Table A:

1. Count: Taken from B.W.M.B. 'Wool Grade Specifications'.
2. Staple: Average length of relaxed fibre.
3. Crimp: For the purposes of this exercise the crimp is expressed as a percentage. Feltmakers will be able to calculate this themselves which will enable them to make comparisons.

    Calculation of % crimp:
    (a) the relaxed fibre length (R)   (c) S - R = E (Extension)
    (b) the stretched fibre length (S)   (d) $\frac{E}{R} \times 100$ = percentage

4. Felting time: Total time taken to achieve felt with maximum shrinkage
5. Shrinkage: Overall difference between batt size and finished felt calculated as a percentage.

Summary of Felt Test Resutls

Breed	Count	Staple	Crimp	Felting Time	Shrinkage
Mountain and Hill Type					
Cheviot	48s - 56s	14cm	7%	31 mins	44%
Derbyshire Gritsone	50s - 56s	6.5cm	23%	20 mins	38%
Exmoor Horn	48s - 54s	12cm	21%	23 mins	43%
Herdwick	28s - 32s	10cm	25%	26 mins	31%
Scottish Blackface	28s - 32s	36cm	3%	26 mins	46%
Welsh Mountain	36s - 48s	8cm	6%	24 mins	48%
White Faced Woodland	50s - 54s	10.5cm	43%	18 mins	27%
Shortwool & Down Type					
Clun Forest	56s - 58s	5.5cm	45%	19 mins	34%
Dorset Down	56s - 58s	8.5cm	24%	26 mins	31%
Dorset Horn	54s - 58s	7.5cm	27%	29 mins	48%
Kerry Hill	52s - 56s	8cm	50%	36 mins	28%
Llanwenog	50s - 56s	6.5cm	30%	31 mins	46%
Ryeland	56s - 58s	4.5cm	56%	24 mins	31%
Shetland	50s - 60s	9cm	55%	18 mins	50%
Suffolk	54s - 58s	6cm	25%	27 mins	15%
Medium Type					
Border Leicester	48s - 52s	15cm	20%	26 mins	30%
Jacob	48s - 56s	11.5cm	30%	27 mins	30%
Romney Marsh	48s - 54s	11cm	32%	27 mins	50%
Texel	46s - 56s	6.5cm	54%	20 mins	31%
Longwool & Lustre					
Blue Faced Leicester	56s - 60s	13cm	23%	20 mins	45%
Lincoln Longwool	36s - 40s	18cm	16%	22 mins	53%
Masham	46s - 50s	14cm	25%	21 mins	39%
Teeswater	44s - 50s	27cm	22%	21 mins	50%
Wensleydale	44s - 50s	27.5cm	21%	19 mins	27%
Fine Wools					
Merino	64s - 100s	6cm	58%	15 mins	50%

Graph A

Relation between count and crimp uses selection of fleece types from count range 30s - 70s
Data taken from table A

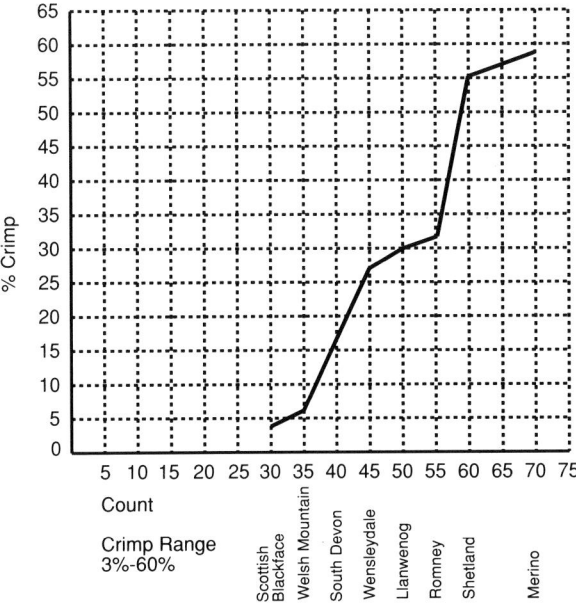

Crimp Range
3%-60%

The Graph shows a clear colleration between the increasing quality count and percentage crimp

Graph B

Relation between count an felting time
data taken from Table A
Examples from count range 30s - 70s as Graph A

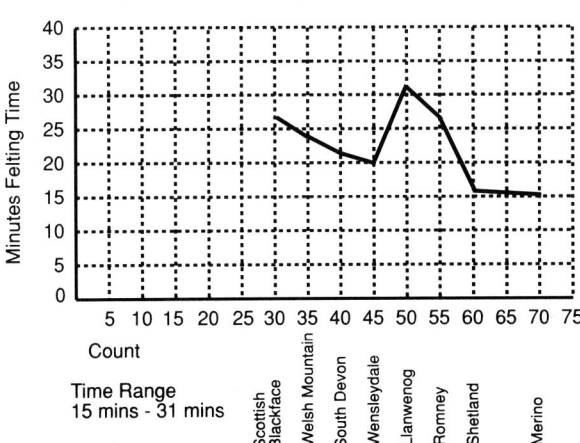

Time Range
15 mins - 31 mins

Graph C

Relation between count and Shrinkage data
taken from Table A
Examples from count range 30s - 70s as Graph A

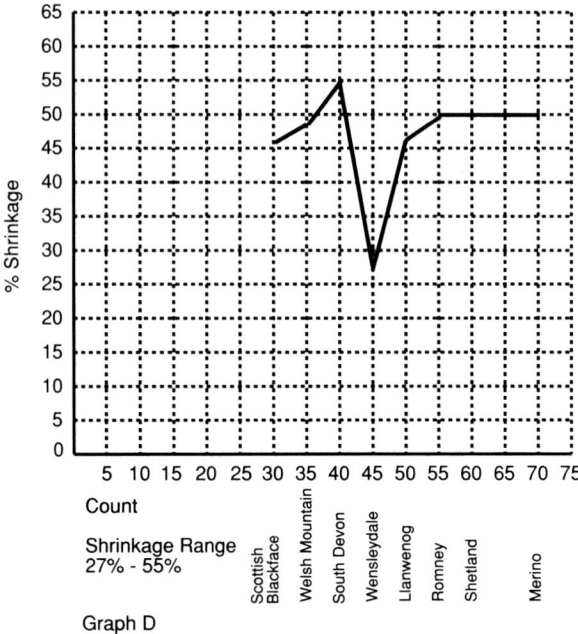

Graph D

Relation between the time taken and shrinkage
data taken from Table A
Examples from count range 30s - 70s as Graph A

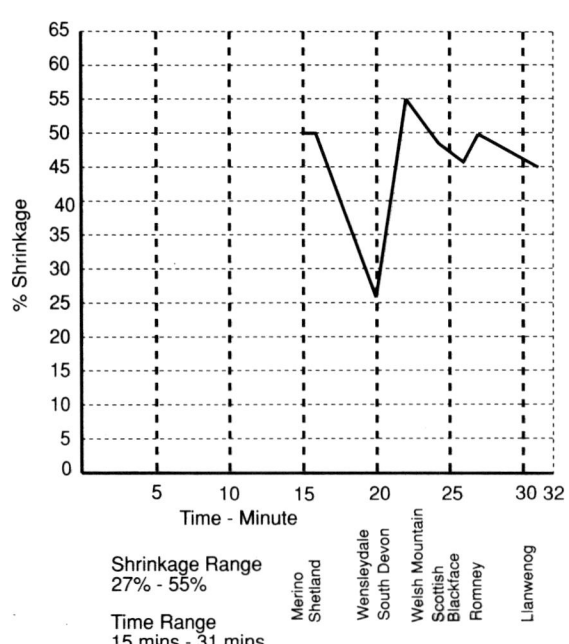

Observations

Graph A clearly shows a relationship between the increasing quality count and percentage crimp of the fibre.

Graph B shows that in general the higher quality fibres felt more quickly than those of a lower count. Llanwenog (30% crimp) and Romney (32% crimp) do not conform to this tendency. Llanwenog takes twice as long to felt as Merino.

Graph C shows an average of 46% shrinkage but again here is an exception. Wensleydale has a 27% shrink factor.

Graph D Wensleydale is again exceptional in the relation between time taken and shrinkage achieved.

Conclusions

Although facts and figures can be a valued source of information and guidance for choosing fleece there seems to be an unknown factor where feltmaking is concerned.

A wise feltmaker will always test a fleece to avoid disappointment with the finished product.

Record Keeping

The best way in which to build up a body of knowledge about your own feltmaking is to keep careful records of fibre type and quantity, methods used and time taken for each piece of felt. If a sample of the finished felt is then attached to the record sheet it becomes a valuable reference for future feltmaking.

It is almost impossible to estimate the quantity of fibre required for a particular project or to state categorically the number of layers which should be laid down unless some sampling has been carried out in advance. The thickness of layers laid down by different feltmakers will vary according to their ability to handle the fibres and, therefore, there cannot be hard-and-fast rules about the number of layers required. This illustrates the importance of each feltmaker keeping records and then decisions can be taken based on samples of their own felt.

Another important point which must be recorded is the amount of shrinkage of each sample. Unless this is known it is not possible to calculate accurately the size of batt required for the particular project. The shrinkage is usually expressed as a percentage - using the starting measurements of the batt and the final measurements of the finished felt to calculate this.

Beginning to keep records: Different types and weights of felt are required for different purposes - for example fine, pliable but well-milled felt is best for a waistcoat or jacket, while felt for hats, bags and slippers needs to be stronger and much firmer and felt for purely decorative purposes can be softer if desired. An experienced feltmaker will be able to produce just the type of felt required for each project.

As a start it would be useful to make at least three samples before starting on a large project. Samples should be made using two, three and four layers of fibres. The results would provide guide-lines as to the number of layers which would be suitable for a particular project.

Sample Record Sheet

Date: ....

Type of fibre: ....

Weight of fibre used: * ....

Measurement of batt: length .... width ....

Direction of first layer ....

Number & colour of layers: ....

Type of decoration: ....

Wetting and setting time: ....

Hardening with dowel: ....

Hardening in mat: ....

Measurements after rolling: length .... width ....

Milling: time taken: ....

Final measurements: length .... width ....

% shrinkage: ....

Description of felt: ....

Further comments: ....

....

....

* To calculate weight of fibre used:

a)   weigh out a generous amount of fibre to begin with

b)   weigh unused fibre

c)   the difference in weight will be the actual weight of fibre used.

A Summary of Technical Information for the Serious Student

Why wool shrinks
Shrinkage of wool is caused by a combination of the physical properties of wool and the physical conditions to which the wool is subjected.

The all-important properties of wool which affect shrinkage are:
1. scaliness of the fibre
2. crimp and curl of the fibre
3. fineness of the fibre
4. length of the fibre

The physical conditions which are required for shrinkage are:
1. Moisture - dry wool never shrinks
2. Agitation
3. Acidity or alkalinity

The effect of these conditions is as follows:
1. Moisture causes wool to relax and stretch more easily.
2. Mechanical action - wool fibres possess the property of unidirectional movement but only if they are pushed, pulled or squeezed. They can only move if subjected to stress or compression and when they move they migrate root end first. This mechanical action can be produced commercially by hammers in milling stocks or squeeze rollers in the rotary milling machine but can also be produced by a domestic washing machine or by hand. The unidirectional movement of wool can be tested quite simply by taking a wool fibre between thumb and forefinger and rubbing them together. The fibre travels and consistently moves with the root end leading. When a fibre is extended under mechanical forces, as in felting the tendency is for the root end to remain in position and pull the tip towards it rather than vice-versa
3. Acidity or alkalinity - another factor which affects the felting of wool is the pH of the solution which is used to wet out wool ready for felting. Wool fibres have a pH 4.9 and at that level are at their most stable with scales lying smooth and flat and are best able to withstand felting. Wool also felts least in neutral or slightly acid conditions and over the range of pH 4 - 7 felting is slow.

Wool fibres stretch and swell more when wet than dry and also more easily in acid or alkaline, rather than neutral solutions. Water is regarded as neutral at pH 7 but the addition of vinegar (dilute acetic acid) will acidify the solution or a small quantity of washing soda will make it alkaline. Wool can be felted successfully in either acid or alkaline conditions but hand feltmakers tend to felt in alkaline conditions adding either soap or detergent to the water and sometimes a little washing soda.

As the pH value rises, the degree of swelling increases until pH 10 when the greatest degree of shrinkage takes place. Above this level the wool fibres can be irreparably damaged especially if the solution is hot.

The addition of soap or detergent to water for use as a felting solution also acts as a lubricant which reduces the friction, facilitates fibre travel and so produces greater shrinkage. Care must be taken, however, not to add to much soap or detergent when making felt by hand as too many suds can have a detrimental effect on the rate of felting.

The graph shows the relationship between pH and shrinkage when hand felting.

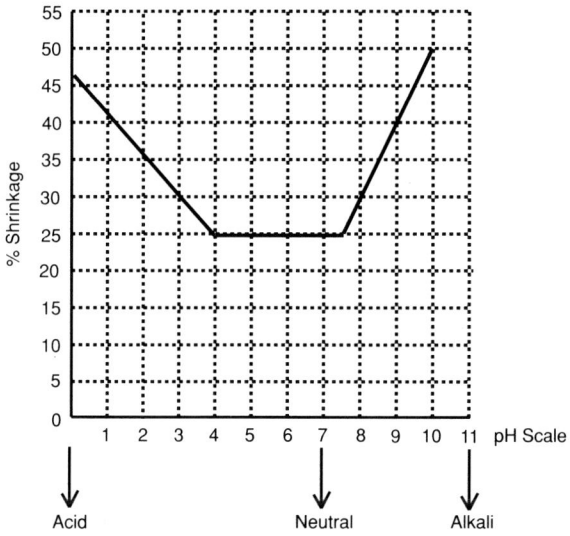

pH 3 - 4 = lemon juice
pH 4.9 = wool fibre
pH 7 = water (neutral)
pH 7 - 8 = soap flakes
pH 9 = washing machine detergent

In industry both acid and alkaline felting processes are used in the milling of woollen cloths. Alkali + soap milling gives a soft handle to the cloth while acid milling gives a stronger cloth and is used for cloths to be made into uniforms where durability is of great importance.

Method of Testing the pH of Felt

Equipment: soil testing kit from a garden centre
5cm square of felt
250ml water, rain or distilled water is preferred and essential if tap water is either very acid or alkaline
small pan
small jug
strainer

Method
1. Cut felt into small pieces.
2. Place pieces in pan with water and boil for 15 minutes.
3. Allow felt to cool in the liquid.
4. Squeeze liquid out of felt and strain into a jug .
5. Follow the directions for testing using the kit:
   (a) Put measured amount of liquid into container
   (b) Add contents of capsule provided.
   (c) Shake thoroughly.
   (d) Allow liquid to settle for several minutes.

Result

The pH shows as a change of colour ranging from green to red on the scale provided. It also enumerates the pH ranging from pH 7.5 (alkaline) to pH 4.5 (acid).

In order of importance the three essential factors in felting are:
1. fibres must have a scale structure
2. fibres must be wet
3. fibres must be moved about

The Properties of Felt
1. Felt does not fray or unravel.
2. It has no warp or weft limitations so is economical in pattern-laying.
3. It can be cut or stamped into any shape.
4. It can be sheared, pressed smooth or lightly brushed.
5. The surface wears evenly as there are no yarns to break.
6. It is easier to separate into layers (i.e. the original formation) than to tear it by pulling lengthways or across the width.
7. It is highly resilient and can be compressed without damage to the fibres.
8. It is less absorbent than fabrics which are woven, knitted etc. and which have an open structure. It can be made waterproof.
9. Because of its compressed structure it is windproof.
10. It has good insulating properties and can withstand extremes of temperature.
11. Finishing agents can be used successfully without loss of quality.
12. Felt retains the characteristics of wool fibres which dye easily and are flame resistant.

The Nature of Felt
Developing a feel for felt is very necessary, as that is a requirement for being able to decide at what stage the felt is completed. The appearance and handle of wool fibres can indicate the description of the finished felt so that the feltmaker should acquire a vocabulary of descriptive words. This information could be added to the 'record sheet' of each felt made.

Suggested vocabulary:

1. coarse	7. hard	13. smooth
2. crisp	8. harsh	14. soft
3. dense	9. kempy	15. spongy
4. dull	10. lustrous	16. springy
5. fine	11. matt	17. variable
6. hairy	12. silky	

Bibliography

ALLAN, RICHARD & BURNS, MARCIA	*Wool Quality - evaluation and improvement.* Richard Allan, Eyemouth 1992
ANLEZARK, MILDRED	*Hats on Heads, The Art of Creative Millinery.* Kangaroo Press Ltd. 1990
BAWDEN, JANET	*The Hat Book - Creating hats for every occasion.* Charles Letts & Co. 1992
BOWDEN, P.J.	*The Regulations of the Internal Wool Trade.* B.W.M.B.
B.W. M. B.	*British Sheep and Wool.* 1990
B.W.M.B.	*Wool Grade Specifications.* 1992
BONNINGTON, CHRIS	*Kongur' - China's Elusive Summit.* Hodder & Stoughton. 1982
BRITISH MUSEUM	*Frozen Tombs. The Culture and Art of the Ancient Tribes of Siberia.* 1978
BURKETT, M. E. O.B.E.	*The Art of the Feltmaker.* Abbot Hall Gallery, Kendal, Cumbria. 1979
COOK, J. GORDON	*Handmade Textile Fibres.* Merrow. 1959 - 68
CATULLUS	*Poems.* c84 - 54 BC
CHADWICK, EILEEN	*The Craft of Handspinning.* Batsford. 1980
COLLIER, ANN M.	*A Handbook of Textiles.* Pergammon Press. 1974
DAVENPORT, ELSIE G.	*Your Handspinning.* Craft & Hobby Bookservice, California.

EVERS, INGE	*Feltmaking Technique and Projects.* A.C.Black. 1987
FANNIN, ALLEN	*Handspinning - Art & Technique.* Van Nostrand Reinhold. 1970
FREEMAN, SUE	*Feltcraft. Handcrafted felt from fleece to finished projects.* David & Charles. 1988
GORDON, BEVERLEY	*Feltmaking , Traditions, techniques and contemporary explorations.* Watson - Guptill Publications. 1980
HALL, A.. J.	*A Students Handbook of Textile Science.* Allman & Son, London. 1969
HARNETT, CYNTHIA	*The Wool-Pack.* Penguin Books. 1951
HEBBLETHWAITE, B.	Poem - Social History. Piece Hall, Halifax.
INTERNATIONAL WOOL SECRETARIAT	*The Book of Wool.* *Wool Science Review 61.* I.W.S. March 1985
MONCRIEFF, R. W.	*Wool Shrinkage and its Prevention.* National Trade Press Ltd. London. 1953
NABNEY, JANET	*Machine Knitted Fabrics - Felting Techniques.* Batsford. 1992
ONIONS, W. J.	*Wool - An introduction to its properties , varieties, uses and production.* Interscience 1962
ROSS, MABEL	*Yarn Design, The Essential for Handspinners.* M. Ross, Kinross . 1982
ROSS, MABEL	*The Encyclopedia of Handspinning.* Batsford, London. also Interweave Press. 1988
RYDER, MICHAEL L.	*Sheep and Wool for Handcraft Workers.* 1978

SCHOFIELD, JOHN & SCHOFIELD, J.COLIN	*The Finishing of Wool Goods.* Published by the authors, Kirkburton, Huddersfield 1935
SPARK, PATRICIA	*Fundamentals of Feltmaking.* Shuttle Craft Books, Coupeville, Washington. 1989
SPARK, PATRICIA	*Scandinavian-Style Feltmaking. A traditional approach to hats, boots and other useful objects.* Shuttle Craft Books Coupeville, Washington. 1992
SPARK, PATRICIA	*Choosing the Fibre for Feltmaking.* Shuttle, Spindle and Dyepot. 1968
WALTER, PETER	*Felt, Techniques, Technology and Tradition.* 1986
WATSON, ANGELA	*Handmade Felt.* an article in Weavers' Journal.
WHITWORTH ART GALLERY	*The Qashqas of Iran.* 1976

Glossary

Batt The preparation stage for feltmaking. Webs of fibres are peeled off hand or drum carders and then layered to form a batt several centimetres in depth. Alternatively short lengths of fibres are pulled from combed tops and placed side by side to form a batt several layers deep.

Blending A process in the preparation of wool fibres when different colours can be carded together for decorative effect. Also used for combining fibres of different characteristics, types or qualities.

Bradford Count The measure of fineness of wool based on the number of hanks of yarn each 560 yards in length which can be worsted spun from one pound weight of wool fibres e.g. if 50 hanks are spun the count is then 50s.

Breeds The generic term used in the classification of sheep which is then sub-divided according to type:- Shortwool and Down, Medium, Longwool and Lustre, Mountain and Hill.

Capeline Large three dimensional felt shaped like a cone which is used for making large-brimmed hats.

Carbonising A commercial process for cleaning wool by treating it with a dilute solution of sulphuric acid to remove any cellulosic parts of bushes and plants picked up by the fleece when the sheep were grazing.

Carding The process of teasing and opening out wool to separate the individual fibres. The result of hand or drum carding is a lap of aligned fibres in preparation for spinning or feltmaking.

Carrotting A commercial process formerly used in the hat-making industry for treating fur fibres to soften them and increase their feltabilty. Originally nitrate of mercury was used but this was poisonous to the hatters and created health problems. The Mad Hatter in 'Alice in Wonderland' was a character based on these facts.

Cellulosic Fibres consisting of cellulose, e.g. cotton, linen, ramie, also regenerated cellulose, e.g. viscose.

Combing	A process after carding which is for the preparation of worsted yarn. The combing process removes the shorter fibres (Noil) leaving the longer fibres to produce a smoother yarn when spun. (see Worsted).
Cone	Three dimensional cone shaped felt used to make small head-hugging or small brimmed hats. (see Hood).
Cortex	Makes up to 90% of the wool fibre. It is made up of millions of cells which provide the strength and elasticity of wool. (see Orthocortex and Paracortex).
Cotted	A description of fleece which has become matted near the skin. The staples of such a fleece are therefore difficult to separate and card.
Count	As for **Bradford Count.** Also known as **Bradford Quality Numbers.**
Crimp	The visual waviness of wool fibres. Crimp varies greatly according to wool quality. It can be measured as crimps per centimetre.
Crossbred	Sheep which have been bred from two or more different breeds over a period of time to improve flesh, fleece or both. Crossbred wool ranges in quality from 46s - 58s.
Cross-Lay	This refers to the method of building up the wool batt which is then felted. Carded layers or layers of combed fibres are placed so that each layer lies at right angles, i.e. across the previous layer.
Density	A general term describing the compactness of felt. More specifically weight per unit volume measured in grams per centimetre.
D.F.E.	**Directional Frictional Effect** The term used to describe the movement of fibres. It is dictated by the scale structure and the fact that wool fibres move in a root-ways direction when subject to friction.
Doffing	The removing of a lap of carded wool fibres from hand or drum carders.

Felt	A generic name given to a fabric where wool fibres are interlocked and entangled. With the application of moisture, heat and friction they are transformed into a compact mass and become felt.
Felting Board	A ridged board used to speed up the milling process in felting.
Feral	The wild state of animals before domestication.
Fibre(s)	Individual hairs which are grown collectively as fleece on sheep. Other animals such as alpaca, camel and cashmere, produce hair fibres. Fibres can be of vegetable origin, e.g. cotton, or synthetic as in nylon. The varying length of the fibre is called the staple. (See Staple)
Fleece	The shorn wool of a sheep. It can mean the whole fleece or a mass of wool fibres.
Fulling	A process which compacts the felt and increases the density by using further friction and heat. (See Milling).
Fur-Felt	Felt traditionally used in hat production made from animal fur, e.g. beaver and muskrat. Fur fibres need chemical preparation before felting. (See Carrotting)
Hair	Can be found as a proportion of fibres within a fleece of lower quality. They are coarser and longer than wool. Commercially Hair Felt is made of hair from cows or goats but is very coarse with limited uses.
Half-Felt	Also known as soft-felt. Fibres which have been cross layered and felted just enough to form a cohesive sheet but which have not begun to shrink. Used for inlay and mosaic techniques in felt design.
Hardening	The continuing process of felting from the soft felt stage to the point where it is cohesive and has become a low ensity felt.
Hood	Used in hatmaking. Also known as a cone. (See Cone).
Inlay	A technique in felt design. Half-felted pieces are cut into shapes, laid on top of a batt of unfelted fibres and the whole is then felted together. The half-felted pieces retain their original shape throughout the process.

Kemp	Short, coarse fibres which appear whitish in colour. They resist dyeing and do not contribute to the strength of felt, tending to remain on the surface.
Keratin	The protein composition of wool fibres. Many different amino acids are linked to form the complex molecules of protein.
Lanolin	The refined fatty substance secreted by the sebaceous glands of the sheep which can be removed by scouring. When purified it can be made into soap. Also known as 'Wool Fat' (See Suint).
Lap	The layer of carded wool from hand or drum carders. This varies in thickness according to the quantity of fleece used. When built up into layers becomes the batt.
Lustre Wools	Examples are Lincoln Longwool, Leicester Longwool, Wensleydale and Cotswold. The staple can be up to 37cm in length. An average fleece weighs about 7 kg. The lustre gives an attractive finish to felt.
Mawata Cap	Degummed and pierced silk cocoons are opened out and stretched in thin layers on a frame. Layers are then built up and finally shaped over an upturned bowl. Single layers can be pulled off and used to decorate the surface of felt.
Medulla	Hollow space running down the centre of a wool fibre. The coarser the fibre the larger the medulla. In most Merino fibres the medulla is either absent or so fine as to be invisible.
Merino	A breed of sheep producing fine wool of 60s count upwards. It is of Spanish origin but thrives in Australia, South Africa and New Zealand. 'English Merino' is now available.
Micron	A measurement of fibre thickness. One micron equals one millionth of a metre. An alternative to the Bradford Count System which is used mainly in the Southern Hemisphere.
Milling	The process after hardening which increases the density of felt. (See Fulling).
Mosaic	Design built up of half-felted pieces fitted together to form an

	all over design. This layer may then be placed on an unfelted batt and the whole felted together - this produces a felt with a flat smooth surface
Mother Felt	A term used in traditional hand-felting to describe a felt used as a cloth. The Batt for a new felt is prepared on it and then rolled in it.
Nap	The hairy surface on some fabrics. Can be created by teasing or brushing the surface. Also refers to the pile of, e.g. velvet.
Needlefelt	A felt which is formed by the mechanical action of a Needleloom. Barbed needles are quickly and repeatedly passed through the batt entangling the fibres.
Neps	Small knots of tangled fibres which cannot be removed by carding. Can become a feature of texture. Remove by hand for a smooth-finished felt.
Noil	Short wool fibres which are removed by combing. This is a necessary preparation for worsted spinning. Noil is very useful in feltmaking and can be blended with longer fibres.
Orthocortex	Part of the Cortex of a wool fibre which is composed of tightly packed cells. (See Cortex and Paracortex)
Paracortex	Part of the Cortex of a wool fibre. The orthocortex and the paracortex form a spiral in the fibre which causes the crimp. (See Cortex and Crimp).
pH	This is the measure of acidity of liquids - pH 7 being neutral. The lower the number e.g. pH 2 is strongly acidic while numbers above pH 7 are increasingly alkaline. Wool is immune to the action of acid / alkali between pH 4 and pH 8. Strong alkali solutions can irreversably damage wool. Felt should have a pH between 5 and 8.
Pressed Felt	Material which is produced by using the inherent property to entangle and shrink, i.e. felt. It is neither woven, bonded by adhesive or manufactured by needling.
Proofing	Treatments given to felt to improve it in use, e.g. mothproofing, waterproofing and flameproofing. Stiffening treatments are also used in hat making.

Quality	The quality of wool is expressed as a number. The higher numbers indicate finer wools, the lower ones coarser grades. Merino could be 60s plus but Herdwick 30s. Average qualities are 48s - 58s.
Rooing	Plucking the soft underwool by hand from the Shetland sheep. This is done when the natural moult begins.
Scales	The distinctive feature of animal fibres which makes the fibre rough in one direction and smooth in the other. Having scales is the characteristic essential for the ability of wool to felt. (See D. F. E. and Fibres).
Scour	The process of removing dirt, grease, suint and vegetable matter from fleece by washing.
Soft Felt	The description of the batt when it is just beginning to mesh together to form a cohesive mass. The stage before hardening begins.
Staple	Generally the term given to the length of fibres but can mean a cluster of fibres also called 'locks'. Staples or locks are used when grading wool for length, texture and coarseness.
Stapler	A person who examines wool staples for quality and thus grades the fleece.
Suint	The animal's sweat which, together with grease, is secreted by the sebaceous glands of the sheep and is removed by scouring. (See lanolin).
Tops	Commercially prepared fibres combed into long strips like a loose rope. The long fibres are parallel, well separated and are ideal for making lightweight felt of high quality.
Woollen	The process of spinning a yarn from both the long and short fibres of a fleece. The whole locks when carded, can be used for feltmaking without other preparation.
Worsted	The result of removing the short fibres when preparing a fleece. After carding the fibres are combed, leaving parallel, smoother fibres. (See Carding, Noil, Woollen).
Yolk	The term given to the sweat (Suint) and grease (Lanolin) secreted by the sebaceous glands of the sheep. It is seen as yellowish particles collected near the skin and is removed by scouring.

Abbreviations   B. W. M. B. -   British Wool Marketing Board.
                    I. W. S. -   International Wool Secretariat

Metrication
Weights and measures as used by the B. W. M. B.
1kg - 2.2046lb.   1cm. - 0.393 inches
1lb - 0.436kg   1 inch - 2.54 centimetres

Cautionary Note
For those handling dirty fleece ——-
Catching tetanus is an extremely remote possibility, but feltmakers should be aware of this problem because of its serious consequences. Anyone with cuts or grazes on the hands should wear protective gloves when feltmaking.

Tetanus is indigenous in soil so gardeners too have this concern. A simple precaution is to be protected with an anti-tetanus vaccine which lasts for ten years.

Useful Addresses

Fibres
Adelaide Walker
2 Mill Yard Workshops
Otley Mill
Ilkley Road
Otley
West Yorkshire
LS21 3JP

Fibrecrafts
Style Cottage
Lower Eashing
Godalming
Surrey
GU7 2QD

Tynsell Handspinners
53 Cross Green Road
Dalton
Huddersfield
Yorkshire
HD5 9XX

Fibrecrafts at Barnehowe
Elterwater
Ambleside
Cumbria
LA22 9HW

Millinery Supplies
Paul Craig Ltd
Unit 3
Wealden Business Park
Farningham Road
Crowborough
East Sussex
TN6 2JR

The London Hat House
7 Kensington Mall
London
W8 4EB

Hat Blocks
Boon and Lane
7 - 11 Taylor Street
Luton
Bedfordshire

Muslins
Whaleys (Bradford) Ltd
Harris Court
Great Horton Road
Bradford
BD7 4WQ

Adhesives
Wey Adhesives Ltd
Unit 2, Milton's yard
Petworth Road
Witley
Godalming
Surrey
GU8 5LH

Dyes

M & R Dyes
Carters
Station Road
Wickham Bishop
Witham
Essex
CM8 3JB

Kemtex Services
Tameside Business Park
Windmill Lane
Denton
Manchester
M34 3QS

Notes